Develop Verbal Reasoning

	Frequently asked questions for adults	2
LESSON 1	Finding hidden words	5
LESSON 2	Filling in the missing three-letter word	9
LESSON 3	Moving a letter to make two new words	13
LESSON 4	Using one letter to finish one word and start another	17
LESSON 5	Completing two pairs of words with the same letter	21
LESSON 6	Forming compound words	25
LESSON 7	Finding opposites	29
LESSON 8	Finding the word which can mean each of those in brackets	37
LESSON 9	Working out the missing letters for each sequence	45
LESSON 10	Solving problems with information	49
LESSON 11	Working out indirect codes for words	56
LESSON 12	Completing number patterns	61
LESSON 13	Calculating number sentences	65
LESSON 14	Solving coded analogies	73
LESSON 15	Finding analogical words	77
LESSON 16	Finding the two words which don't belong in the group	81
LESSON 17	Working out the missing codes for each word	89
LESSON 18	Completing the third pair of words using the same pattern	97
LESSON 19	Finding the second word using those outside the brackets	105
LESSON 20	Using the numbers outside the brackets to find the one inside	113
	Score sheet	120
	Vocabulary builder 1: new words	121
	Vocabulary builder 2: problems to solve	123
	Vocabulary builder 3: diminutives	124
	And finally...	125
	Vocabulary builder answers	126
	Answers	127

Frequently Asked Questions For Adults

What is this book about?

Develop Verbal Reasoning is in level two of the *Practise & Pass 11+* series. It is a workbook for students who are going to take an 11+ test or school entrance exam that includes a verbal reasoning section. In it I help students further their knowledge of 11 key types of question they've already practised in level one of the series, and introduce them to 9 new question types that they may face in the test. I also provide 280 further original questions for them to practise.

I provide coaching for students throughout the text. I talk them through the whole process from answering questions to helping them understand their mistakes, so that they have a firm understanding of the basics.

(Note: if they haven't already, I highly recommend that your student work through level one of the series – Discover Verbal Reasoning – before starting this book.)

What is verbal reasoning?

Verbal reasoning is problem-solving using language, vocabulary and sometimes mathematical skills. There are many different type of verbal reasoning question and this book looks at 20 of the most common.

How do I use this book?

This book is divided into bite-sized lessons for the student to work through. Each lesson covers a specific type of question and is set up in the same way:

1. I explain the question type, giving the student an understanding of what they need to know.

2. I provide a worked example or two to show how the question type is best tackled.

   (Note: I do recommend that an adult reads through the explanation and example(s) with the student to ensure they have a firm understanding of what is required.)

3. When ready, the student should work through the first set of practice questions on their own and mark their answers on the answer sheet provided.

   Important: unlike in level one, an adult should mark this set of questions, and all the questions in this book. The answers can be found on pages 127 and 128. You might want to cut these out of the book so the temptation for the student to take a peek is removed!

4. I provide a summary of what the student's score means and give hints on how to improve it, if needs be, and how to speed up their work.

   (Note: the student should discuss any errors and talk through the hints together with an adult so that any problems are dealt with straight away.)

5. In the 9 lessons where I introduce question types that are new to this book there is a second set of practice questions. I suggest that the student shouldn't work on these until they understand why they made mistakes first-time around.

6. Finally, there is a score sheet on page 120 which should be completed after each lesson to keep a record of progress. This can be used to identify those question types the student needs to practise more.

   (Note: occasionally I will include a question that hasn't been explained in the lesson. This is by design: the student will very likely come up against a question they are not familiar with in the actual test so it's important that they get used to applying the knowledge they have to work out the right answer.)

Why does this book feature multiple choice answers?

Multiple choice answers are becoming the most common format for the 11+. This means that four or five possible answers are given for each question and they are presented to the student in a grid format. To answer the question correctly the student has to put a horizontal line in the empty box next to the correct answer.

⇨ It's important that students learn to use these answer grids correctly from the outset so they avoid making common errors, such as marking the wrong box or accidentally missing out questions, that will cause them to lose a mark.

⇨ You should make sure you find out from the examination centre whether the multiple choice format will be used in the final exam so you're confident that the student is doing the right preparation.

When should the student start to prepare for the exam and how often should they practise?

The sooner the student starts to prepare for the exam the better. Realistically, I suggest there should be a full year's run-up to the test so that the student has a chance to practise as many of the subject areas and question types that might appear in the exam as possible without having to study for hours and hours each week. This means working through all three levels of the *Practise & Pass 11+* series (this book is in level two of the series) at a steady and realistic pace.

For this book I recommend students work at the pace of two lessons a week which means 10 weeks in total. However, if a student is able, there is nothing to stop them moving through the book at a quicker pace.

What's the best way for a student to study?

⇨ It's important that the student gets used to a test-type environment so make sure there's a clear space to work in, with no distractions. The TV and any music should be switched off, the student should be sat at a table and there should be a clock in clear view so that they can time themselves.

⇨ Students should use a pencil to answer the questions and have an eraser and some scrap paper to hand which they can use for any workings out.

(Note: I highly recommend that the student avoid practising on the same days that they have school homework and that they also have other extra-curricular activities – this means they have other outlets for their energies and don't become overworked, stressed or too bored with the practice.)

How quickly should a student answer the questions?

As this book is in level two of the series, students should now be used to most of the question types so I do expect them to get up to speed. They should follow the timings I have provided so that they work at a 'real time' pace. I have provided 'tips for speeding up' throughout the book to help with this. Typically in the actual exam they will have 50 minutes to answer 85 verbal reasoning questions (although, do check this with the examination centre as timings can vary).

What score should the student be aiming for?

Remember that 11+ tests and entrance exams are tough to pass. I have written this book to reflect that fact, so it is unlikely that the student will sail through the book scoring 100% in each lesson.

After the first set of practice questions in every lesson I have given a target score for that particular question type – this is based on my experience of teaching them year on year and should help in assessing how the student is doing, and what areas, if any, need work. I also include helpful hints on how students can improve, and would recommend they use the 'vocabulary builders'.

I should add that the scores here in no way indicate whether the student will definitely pass or fail the exam; they are only here as a guide.

What are the 'vocabulary builders'?

There are vocabulary builder exercises in this book which are extra tasks to help improve the student's vocabulary. In addition to these, one of the best ways for students to help prepare for the examination is to read regularly. The better their vocabulary, the better they are likely to cope with the questions in the actual exam.

What should I do once this book is completed?

I recommend that the student move on to level three of the series: *Practice Tests*. This provides full practice test papers for them to work through so that they know exactly what to expect on test day.

LESSON 1 Finding Hidden Words

In this exercise you need to find the four-letter word that's hidden in each sentence. The word will be formed from the letters at the end of one word and the beginning of the next. Remember from the level one book in the series that letters must remain in the same order and that a word found entirely in one word isn't a correct answer. Let's look at an example.

Example

They played happily until evening came.

The answer is tile since it is formed using the letters from two words and it is four letters long. But remember, on your answer sheet you'll have to mark the two words that the word is formed from so, until and evening.

TIP FOR SPEEDING UP

After reading the questions, go straight to the answer sheet. Look at the two words that make up each answer choice. Try to find a hidden word in each of the answer choices. This will save you time as it means you won't have to find your answer on the question paper and then transfer it to the answer sheet. Try it and see how much time you save!

LESSON 1 PRACTICE TEST

My Time

My Score

Now work through the questions below. Go as quickly as you can but make sure you finish them all. When you've found the two words in which the four-letter word is hidden, mark your answers on the opposite page. When you've finished write down the time you took and your score in the boxes above. Remember to ask an adult to mark your answers.

You have six minutes to complete this task, so work quickly!

1. Yesterday he left his bicycle outside.

2. The happy, playful dog rolled over.

3. His wife arrived on the train.

4. The girl smiles sweetly at dinner.

5. He called his brother after work.

6. They played games happily after lunch.

7. The farmer bought six new hens.

8. He was singing early one morning.

9. The children like entering painting competitions.

10. People love visiting the skating rink.

LESSON 1 PRACTICE TEST: ANSWER SHEET

Mark your answer by putting a horizontal line in one of the boxes, as in the example below.

Example:

```
They played     ☐
played happily  ☐
happily until   ☐
until evening   ▬
evening came    ☐
```

1
```
yesterday he    ☐
he left         ☐
left his        ☐
his bicycle     ☐
bicycle outside ☐
```

2
```
the happy      ☐
happy playful  ☐
playful dog    ☐
dog rolled     ☐
rolled over    ☐
```

3
```
his wife     ☐
wife arrived ☐
arrived on   ☐
on the       ☐
the train    ☐
```

4
```
the girl       ☐
girl smiles    ☐
smiles sweetly ☐
sweetly at     ☐
at dinner      ☐
```

5
```
he called    ☐
called his   ☐
his brother  ☐
brother after ☐
after work   ☐
```

6
```
they played    ☐
played games   ☐
games happily  ☐
happily after  ☐
after lunch    ☐
```

7
```
the farmer    ☐
farmer bought ☐
bought six    ☐
six new       ☐
new hens      ☐
```

8
```
she was        ☐
was singing    ☐
singing early  ☐
early one      ☐
one morning    ☐
```

9
```
the children          ☐
children like         ☐
like entering         ☐
entering painting     ☐
painting competitions ☐
```

10
```
people love    ☐
love visiting  ☐
visiting the   ☐
the skating    ☐
skating rink   ☐
```

How Did You Do? Let's Find Out!

Remember, there is no self-marking in this book. Please get an adult to mark your answers.

If you scored 8 or more out of 10

Great work! But do check the words you got wrong to help you understand where your mistakes were.

If you scored fewer than 8 out of 10

⇨ You should know all the words in the questions. If you don't, try spending more time reading to help improve your vocabulary. Also use vocabulary builder 1 (page 121). It will help you to look up new words in a dictionary and practise using them in a sentence of your own.

⇨ Did you spell any words wrongly? If so make a note of any words you got wrong and learn the correct spellings.

⇨ Do you understand what you have to do? If not, ask an adult to read the instructions and go through the example with you again. Then take another look at your answers and see if you can correct them.

⇨ Do you understand how to mark your answers on the answer sheet? Make sure you do this properly as you'll have to understand this on test day. Look at the example on the answer sheet to remind yourself of how to do this.

⇨ Watch out for letters that change their sound when put together. I might have included a few of these just to keep you on your toes!

⇨ Did you think of names or proper nouns as your answer? Remember a proper noun is the specific name of a person, place or thing. Also avoid thinking of names of products too, for example names of shops, cars, and brand names of clothes or food. They're also proper nouns.

LESSON 2 Filling in the Missing Three-Letter Word

In this exercise you'll see a word in CAPITAL letters which has been shortened by removing three of its letters. You'll need to work out which three letters have been removed. These letters will spell a word and this three-letter word is your answer. Remember, the three-letter word should be used as it is spelled – no letters should be rearranged.

Let's look at an example.

Example

The artist created a truly INCIBLE painting.

In this sentence, the word INCIBLE is not correct. Try to think what the word should be. Of course the word should be INCREDIBLE. The missing word is RED. That is the answer you must mark on your answer sheet.

TIPS FOR SPEEDING UP

- If you've got an idea of what the word should be but aren't sure if it is correct, look at the answer choices on the multiple choice grid first. See which one would fit into the word in capitals to make a new word.

- This method will also help you if you have no idea what the word should be or to double check that your idea is right.

LESSON 2 PRACTICE TEST

My Time

My Score

Now look at the questions below. Try to do each one as quickly as you can but make sure you finish them all. When you've found the answer, mark it on the opposite page. When you've finished write down the time you took and your score in the boxes above. Remember to ask an adult to mark your answers.

You have six minutes to complete this task, so work quickly!

1. The wonderful statue was truly RESSIVE.

2. The children took part in a sport COMITION.

3. TORY is a subject at school which looks at the past.

4. The surgeon was extremely CFUL when performing the operation.

5. Every Wednesday my friend goes to piano PRACT.

6. At the end of the year the teachers and children had a great CELEBION at school.

7. 'Are you going to Sam's birthday PY?'

8. At the weekend my parents like to read the NEWSPR.

9. When I looked out of the DOW I could see a pretty bird.

10. One of my hobbies is playing games on my COMER.

LESSON 2 PRACTICE TEST: ANSWER SHEET

Mark your answer by putting a horizontal line in one of the boxes, as in the example below.

Example:

```
ADD  ☐
RID  ☐
RED  ▬
ROD  ☐
ODD  ☐
```

1
```
RAG  ☐
IMP  ☐
BAD  ☐
ARM  ☐
EAR  ☐
```

2
```
PAT  ☐
PIT  ☐
POT  ☐
PUT  ☐
PET  ☐
```

3
```
END  ☐
HER  ☐
HIS  ☐
OUR  ☐
PAT  ☐
```

4
```
CUP  ☐
ARE  ☐
OUR  ☐
ORE  ☐
EAR  ☐
```

5
```
ICE  ☐
HIS  ☐
ACE  ☐
ANT  ☐
AND  ☐
```

6
```
ROT  ☐
RAN  ☐
RUN  ☐
RAT  ☐
RAY  ☐
```

7
```
RAT  ☐
ROT  ☐
ARE  ☐
ATE  ☐
ART  ☐
```

8
```
PAY  ☐
APE  ☐
PAN  ☐
PEN  ☐
PIN  ☐
```

9
```
WIN  ☐
WON  ☐
ONE  ☐
WET  ☐
INN  ☐
```

10
```
PAT  ☐
PET  ☐
PIT  ☐
POT  ☐
PUT  ☐
```

How Did You Do? Let's Find Out!

Remember, there is no self-marking in this book. Please get an adult to mark your answers.

If you scored 8 or more out of 10

Great work! But do make sure you understand where you went wrong if you scored 8 or 9.

If you scored fewer than 8 out of 10

⇨ If you don't know all of the words in the test, try spending more time reading to help improve your vocabulary. Also use the vocabulary builder on page 121 to help you.

⇨ If the instructions are unclear to you ask an adult to explain them. Then take another look at your answers and see if you can correct them.

⇨ Remember the three-letter word must not be changed in any way and it can be missing from anywhere in the word in CAPITALS, including at the front or at the end.

⇨ Finally, if you didn't recognise some of the words or you misspelled them, practise your spelling and make sure you understand the meaning of the words.

LESSON 3 Moving a Letter to Make Two New Words

In this exercise you'll begin with two words. The aim is to remove one letter from the first word and place it into the second word. When you've done this correctly, two new words will be made. You'll need to put a mark next to the correct letter on your answer grid.

Let's look at an example.

Example

stark   sill

First look at the word on the left. Take one letter away at a time and check whether the remaining letters make a word. With 'stark' you can see if you take away...

's' it leaves tark – that's not a word
't' it leaves sark – that's not a word
'a' it leaves strk – that's not a word
'r' it leaves stak – that's not a word
'k' it leaves star – great – that is a word.

Now let's see where that 'k' goes in the second word.

ksill   skill   sikll   silkl   sillk

Looking at these you can see the word 'skill' is a proper word so clearly the letter you should mark on your answer sheet is the k as that is the only one you can move to make two new words.

Remember that your answer can't be a proper noun or a name like 'Stan'.

TIPS FOR SPEEDING UP

- Work methodically starting with the first letter of the first word.

- You can usually ignore vowels that stand alone in the middle of a word – the word most probably won't make sense without them. In the example above, the 'a' in stark is absolutely necessary for the word to work. This approach can save you some time.

LESSON 3 PRACTICE TEST

My Time

My Score

Now work through the questions below. Try to do each one as quickly as you can but make sure you finish them all. When you've found the answer, mark it on the answer sheet opposite. When you've finished write down the time you took and your score in the boxes above. Remember to get an adult to mark your answers.

You have six minutes to complete this task, so work quickly!

1. brake   light
2. barge   room
3. bring   stale
4. likes   spars
5. clamp   feet
6. thigh   plea
7. whose   rings
8. three   bus
9. times   arch
10. dream   arts

LESSON 3 PRACTICE TEST: ANSWER SHEET

Mark your answer by putting a horizontal line in one of the boxes, as in the example below.

Example:

```
s □
t □
a □
r □
k ▬
```

1
```
b □
r □
a □
k □
e □
```

2
```
b □
a □
r □
g □
e □
```

3
```
b □
r □
i □
n □
g □
```

4
```
l □
i □
k □
e □
s □
```

5
```
c □
l □
a □
m □
p □
```

6
```
t □
h □
i □
g □
h □
```

7
```
w □
h □
o □
s □
e □
```

8
```
t □
h □
r □
e □
e □
```

9
```
t □
i □
m □
e □
s □
```

10
```
d □
r □
e □
a □
m □
```

How Did You Do? Let's Find Out!

Remember, there is no self-marking in this book. Please get an adult to mark your answers.

If you scored 8 or more out of 10

This is a great score, well done! Remember to look at the words you got wrong to help you avoid making these mistakes next time.

If you scored fewer than 8 out of 10

⇨ You should know all the words in the questions. If you don't, try spending more time reading to help improve your vocabulary. Use the vocabulary builder on page 121 to help you.

⇨ Did you spell any words wrongly? Read regularly and make a list of any new words you come across and look them up in a dictionary. This way you'll learn what they mean and how to spell them.

⇨ Did you think of names or proper nouns as your answer? Remember these don't count as answers.

⇨ If you don't understand what you need to do, ask an adult to read the instructions and go through the example with you again. Then take another look at your answers and see if you can correct them. Remember when you take the letter from the first word, it must leave behind a real word. Then when you place it in the second word, it must also make another real word.

⇨ Remember that you shouldn't change the order of any of the other letters to make the new word.

LESSON 4 Using One Letter to Finish One Word and Start Another

In this exercise you'll need to find just <u>one</u> letter to finish the word on the left and begin the word on the right so that two new words are formed.

Let's look at an example.

Example

       char   (?)   hump

Which letter will go on the end of char and the beginning of hump to make two new words?

The letter is <u>t</u> which makes char<u>t</u> and <u>t</u>hump

HELPFUL HINTS

- Notice that it's only one letter you need to find.

- You must make two new words and they must be real words, not made up ones!

- If you get completely stuck, don't waste time – move on. Come back to tricky questions at the end.

TIP FOR SPEEDING UP

Go straight to the answers on the multiple choice grid. Look at the five choices – then just try each of these letters to see which one works. This way you don't have to go through the entire alphabet!

LESSON 4 PRACTICE TEST

My Time

My Score

Now work through the questions below. Try to do each one as quickly as you can but make sure you finish them all. When you've found the answer, mark it on the answer sheet opposite. When you've finished write down the time you took and your score in the boxes above. Remember to get an adult to mark your answers.

You have six minutes to complete this task, so work quickly.

1. her   (?)   rink
2. ever   (?)   our
3. slum   (?)   ride
4. shin   (?)   vent
5. ear   (?)   ape
6. pear   (?)   eaves
7. her   (?)   pens
8. care   (?)   each
9. fire   (?)   tale
10. vie   (?)   hole

LESSON 4 PRACTICE TEST: ANSWER SHEET

Mark your answer by putting a horizontal line in one of the boxes, as in the example below.

Example:

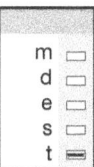

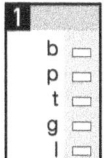 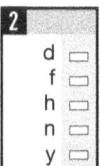 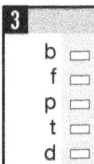 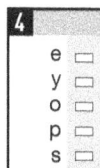

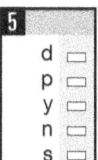   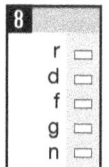

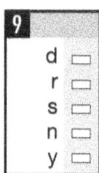 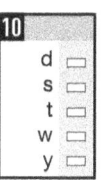

How Did You Do? Let's Find Out!

Remember, there is no self-marking in this book. Please get an adult to mark your answers.

If you scored 8 or more out of 10

Well done, this is a good score. Make sure you understand why you got some answers wrong though.

If you scored fewer than 8 out of 10

⇨ You should know all the words in the questions. If you don't, try spending more time reading to help improve your vocabulary.

⇨ Did you spell any words incorrectly? If you find you're spelling fairly common words wrongly, you'll need to spend more time practising them.

⇨ If you weren't sure what you needed to do, ask an adult to explain the instructions to you. Then take another look at your answers and see if you can correct them. Remember that you are looking for just one letter that will work for both words.

LESSON 5 Completing Two Pairs of Words with the Same Letter

In this exercise, you'll need to work out which letter completes the first word and begins the second. The same letter must also be used to complete the second pair of incomplete words.

Let's look at an example.

Example

car (?) eat   see (?) lay

In this case the missing letter is p which makes the words car**p**, **p**eat, see**p** and **p**lay.

Although some other letters could be used to complete some of the words above, no other letter <u>on the answer grid</u> will work for all of them.

TIP FOR SPEEDING UP

Once again you can use the multiple choice answer grid to help you. Simply look at the five choices there and try each one in turn. That way you don't have to try all the letters of the alphabet, and you won't lose your place on the answer sheet!

LESSON 5 PRACTICE TEST

My Time

My Score

Now look at the questions below. Try to do each one as quickly as you can but make sure you finish them all. When you've finished write down the time you took in the box above. Remember to get an adult to mark your answers. Then mark your score in the box at the top of this page too.

You have six minutes to complete this task, so work quickly.

1. ran (?) its   tan (?) erb
2. slop (?) vent   scar (?) bony
3. shaw (?) imp   sea (?) unch
4. win (?) lee   stron (?) lance
5. stor (?) edal   fir (?) ince
6. spur (?) ense   gran (?) here
7. thro (?) inch   flo (?) heel
8. wan (?) ish   stan (?) rift
9. bat (?) ost   pit (?) ole
10. blis (?) hake   mes (?) tiff

LESSON 5 PRACTICE TEST: ANSWER SHEET

Mark your answer by putting a horizontal line in one of the boxes, as in the example below.

Example:

```
d ☐
t ☐
m ☐
p ▬
n ☐
```

1
```
e ☐
h ☐
j ☐
g ☐
k ☐
```

2
```
f ☐
s ☐
e ☐
a ☐
o ☐
```

3
```
e ☐
r ☐
s ☐
t ☐
l ☐
```

4
```
g ☐
f ☐
e ☐
s ☐
k ☐
```

5
```
d ☐
e ☐
p ☐
m ☐
s ☐
```

6
```
s ☐
n ☐
w ☐
e ☐
t ☐
```

7
```
b ☐
p ☐
s ☐
w ☐
t ☐
```

8
```
e ☐
d ☐
g ☐
w ☐
f ☐
```

9
```
l ☐
s ☐
e ☐
n ☐
h ☐
```

10
```
s ☐
t ☐
y ☐
h ☐
m ☐
```

How Did You Do? Let's Find Out!

Remember, there is no self-marking in this book. Please get an adult to mark your answers.

If you scored 8 or more out of 10

I think these are tricky questions, so well done! If you got any wrong, do look at them again to help you understand why you made mistakes.

If you scored fewer than 8 out of 10

⇨ You should be able to form all four words correctly in these questions. If you can't, try spending more time reading to help improve your vocabulary.

⇨ Did you spell any words wrongly? If you did, go back and make sure you learn how to spell them correctly.

⇨ Do you understand what you have to do? If not, ask an adult to read the instructions and go through the example with you again. Then take another look at your answers and see if you can correct them. Remember that you are looking for just one letter which will work for <u>all four</u> words.

LESSON 6 Forming Compound Words

In this exercise you're given two sets of words. You'll need to choose a word from each set, which, when put together, will form one completely new word. You must then mark both words on your answer grid.

Remember, the word from the top group always comes first in the new word. Also, you mustn't add, remove or change the order of any letters.

Let's look at an example.

Example

arm	leg	head
light	step	time

Work through the words methodically, starting with the words in the top group first.

So in the example above you would start by trying to make a word beginning with 'arm'. You could make;

arm + light =	armlight	But that's not a word!
arm + step =	armstep	But that's not a word!
arm + time =	armtime	But that's not a word!

So you move along to the next word;

leg + light =	leglight	But that's not a word!
leg + step =	legstep	But that's not a word!
leg + time =	legtime	But that's not a word!

So you try the last one;

head + light =	headlight	Now that is a word!

So you would mark the words <u>head</u> and <u>light</u> on your answer grid.

TIPS FOR SPEEDING UP

Once again you can look straight at the answer grid to speed up your search. If you aren't sure which answer is right, write out the choices on a piece of scrap paper to see if they work.

LESSON 6 PRACTICE TEST

My Time

My Score

Now look at the questions below. Try to do each one as quickly as you can but make sure you finish them all. When you've found the answer mark it on the answer sheet. When you've finished write down the time you took and your score in the boxes above. Remember to get an adult to mark your answers.

You have six minutes to complete this task, so work quickly!

1 big   long   cup
     board   time   saucer

2 war   new   loud
     noise   den   king

3 then   than   think
     now   more   king

4 great   men   card
     things ace   time

5 car   bar   old
     rage   wheel   door

6 thank   more   skill
     less   full   them

7 wide   draw   short
     road   paper   bridge

8 tree   new   our
     house   garden turn

9 this   same   ramp
     time   age   car

10 nest   bird   tall
     branch tree   led

LESSON 6 PRACTICE TEST: ANSWER SHEET

Mark your answer by putting a horizontal line in one of the boxes for each set of words, as in the example below.

Example:

arm ☐	light ▬
leg ☐	step ☐
head ▬	time ☐

1
big ☐	board ☐
long ☐	time ☐
cup ☐	saucer ☐

2
war ☐	noise ☐
new ☐	den ☐
loud ☐	king ☐

3
then ☐	now ☐
than ☐	more ☐
think ☐	king ☐

4
great ☐	things ☐
men ☐	ace ☐
card ☐	time ☐

5
car ☐	rage ☐
bar ☐	wheel ☐
old ☐	door ☐

6
thank ☐	less ☐
more ☐	full ☐
skill ☐	them ☐

7
wide ☐	road ☐
draw ☐	paper ☐
short ☐	bridge ☐

8
tree ☐	house ☐
new ☐	garden ☐
our ☐	turn ☐

9
this ☐	time ☐
same ☐	age ☐
ramp ☐	car ☐

10
nest ☐	branch ☐
bird ☐	tree ☐
tall ☐	led ☐

How Did You Do? Let's Find Out!

Remember, there is no self-marking in this book. Please get an adult to mark your answers.

If you scored 7 or more out of 10

Great work! Do make sure you understand where you went wrong to help you improve next time.

If you scored fewer than 7 out of 10

⇨ You should know all the words in the questions. If you don't, try to read at home every evening to help improve your vocabulary. You can also use the vocabulary builder on page 121 to help you.

⇨ Did you put words together which made sense but didn't actually make one new compound word? Be careful not to do this. For example in question 5 'car' and 'door' make sense together as 'car door' but do not make one word, so this is not a correct answer.

⇨ Ask an adult to read the instructions and go through the example with you again. Then take another look at your answers and see if you can correct them. Remember you must choose a word from the first group first and then choose one from the second group.

⇨ Remember that you aren't permitted to choose two words from the same group.

LESSON 7 Finding Opposites

This is a question type that you didn't work on in the level one book in the series, so I have added extra questions here for practise.

In these questions you are given two sets of words. You need to choose a word from each set which are <u>opposite</u> in meaning (opposites are also known as antonyms). You must always choose one word from the first group, and one from the second group.

Example

rise	insect	leap
speed	fall	soar

The answer to the example above should be <u>rise</u> from the first group and <u>fall</u> from the second group.

TIP FOR SPEEDING UP

- Once you know that you're looking for opposites you could go straight to the answer sheet since it will contain the same words as the questions. It will save you time and you won't lose your place on the answer sheet.

- Build up your vocabulary so you know what words mean. This will allow you to spot opposites more quickly.

LESSON 7 PART 1

My Time

My Score

Now work through the questions below. When you think you have found both words mark them on the answer sheet on the opposite page. You have six minutes to complete this task, so work quickly.

When you have finished write your time in the box at the top.

1	happy	bitter	miserable
	lemon	chocolate	sweet
2	here	remain	depart
	leave	arrive	welcome
3	plain	interesting	testing
	easy	peculiar	average
4	truth	reference	uncertain
	fiction	science	unsure
5	rainy	glossy	grey
	dull	glittering	dark
6	identical	uneven	rough
	similar	craggy	different
7	early	recently	delayed
	punctual	never	soon
8	whisper	giggle	despair
	sing	sob	croak
9	brittle	harsh	fragile
	tender	hard	tough
10	loud	muffled	echo
	noisy	clear	sound

30

LESSON 7 PART 1: ANSWER SHEET

Mark your answer by putting a horizontal line in one of the boxes for each set of words, as in the example below.

Example:

rise ▬	speed ☐
insect ☐	fall ▬
leap ☐	soar ☐

1

happy ☐	lemon ☐
bitter ☐	chocolate ☐
miserable ☐	sweet ☐

2

here ☐	leave ☐
remain ☐	arrive ☐
depart ☐	welcome ☐

3

plain ☐	easy ☐
interesting ☐	peculiar ☐
testing ☐	average ☐

4

truth ☐	fiction ☐
reference ☐	science ☐
uncertain ☐	unsure ☐

5

rainy ☐	dull ☐
glossy ☐	glittering ☐
grey ☐	dark ☐

6

identical ☐	similar ☐
uneven ☐	craggy ☐
rough ☐	different ☐

7

early ☐	punctual ☐
recently ☐	never ☐
delayed ☐	soon ☐

8

whisper ☐	sing ☐
giggle ☐	sob ☐
despair ☐	croak ☐

9

brittle ☐	tender ☐
harsh ☐	hard ☐
fragile ☐	tough ☐

10

loud ☐	noisy ☐
muffled ☐	clear ☐
echo ☐	sound ☐

How Did You Do? Let's Find Out!

Remember, there is no self-marking in this book. Please get an adult to mark your answers.

If you scored 7 or more out of 10

This is a great score but do look at the questions you got wrong to help you improve.

If you scored fewer than 7 out of 10

⇨ You should be able to work out which words are opposites. If you can't then you should spend more time reading to help improve your vocabulary. Use the vocabulary builder on page 121 to write down new words and learn what they mean.

⇨ Do you understand what you have to do? If not, ask an adult to re-read the instructions and go through the example with you again. Then take another look at your answers and see if you can correct them. Remember you must choose a word from the first group first and then choose one from the second group.

⇨ Remember that you are not permitted to choose two words from the same group.

LESSON 7 PART 2

My Time

My Score

Now look at the questions below. When you think you have found both words mark them on the answer sheet. You have six minutes to complete this task so work quickly.

When you have finished write your time and score in the box at the top.

1. taste   rabble   nibble
   gobble   touch   drink

2. success   win   prize
   failure   medal   attempt

3. supply   store   purchase
   find   provide   withold

4. plane   soft   craggy
   smooth   calm   rocky

5. serious   cheerful   bored
   nervous   miserable tired

6. broad   squat   heavy
   miniscule rotund   tall

7. lumpy   tremble   sloppy
   uneven   solid   boiling

8. endure   communicate commence
   complete unfinished continue

9. aloud   permitted premise
   bidding. forbidden allowed

10. stain   staying   colour
    clean   clearing   reduce

34

LESSON 7 PART 2: ANSWER SHEET

Mark your answer by putting a horizontal line in one of the boxes for each set of words, as in the example below.

Example:

rise ▬	speed ☐
insect ☐	fall ▬
leap ☐	soar ☐

1

taste ☐	gobble ☐
rabble ☐	touch ☐
nibble ☐	drink ☐

2

success ☐	failure ☐
win ☐	medal ☐
prize ☐	attempt ☐

3

supply ☐	find ☐
store ☐	provide ☐
purchase ☐	withold ☐

4

plane ☐	smooth ☐
soft ☐	calm ☐
craggy ☐	rocky ☐

5

serious ☐	nervous ☐
cheerful ☐	miserable ☐
bored ☐	tired ☐

6

broad ☐	miniscule ☐
squat ☐	rotund ☐
heavy ☐	tall ☐

7

lumpy ☐	uneven ☐
tremble ☐	solid ☐
sloppy ☐	boiling ☐

8

endure ☐	complete ☐
communicate ☐	unfinished ☐
commence ☐	continue ☐

9

aloud ☐	bidding ☐
permitted ☐	forbidden ☐
premise ☐	allowed ☐

10

stain ☐	clean ☐
staying ☐	clearing ☐
colour ☐	reduce ☐

LESSON 8 Finding the Word Which Can Mean Each of Those in the Brackets

This is another question type that you haven't seen before, so I have included two sets of questions here for practise.

In these questions you are given two pairs of words which are in brackets. You are then given five further words. You need to choose one word from these five, which could be used in place of all of those in the brackets.

Let's look at an example.

Example

                (shatter, destroy)   (rest, pause)

sleep   disturb   injure   break   wait

The answer to the example above is <u>break</u> since this could mean to destroy or shatter something and it could also mean a rest or pause.

HELPFUL HINTS

- Check each word in turn to see if it could mean the same as each pair. As soon as you think it cannot, cross it out and move onto the next word.

- You really must consider all the meanings of words so try to look at them and think of the different ways they might be used.

LESSON 8 PART 1

My Time

My Score

Now work through the questions below. When you think you have found the word mark it on the answer sheet. You have six minutes to complete this task, so work quickly.

When you have finished write your time and score in the boxes above.

1   (route, path)   (follow, track)
road   watch   trail   lane   cycle

2   (novel, tome)   (reserve, arrange)
leaflet   book   organise   read   visit

3   (number, figure)   (finger, thumb)
shape   calculate   toe   hand   digit

4   (container, chest)   (example, sample)
bag   box   show   case   explain

5   (pluck, hold)   (clasp, hook)
catch   grab   take   barb   snatch

6   (pledge, give)   (present, donation)
generous   gift   sell   charity   help

7   (equal, uniform)   (flat, smooth)
calm   balanced   same   soft   even

8   (boat, ship)   (bring, carry)
hold   tanker   vessel   ferry   sail

9   (write, note)   (scrap, shred)
jot   letter   part   tear   paper

10   (retain, hold)   (fort, castle)
grasp   palace   tower   keep   secure

LESSON 8 PART 1: ANSWER SHEET

Mark your answer by putting a horizontal line in one of the boxes, as in the example below.

Example:

sleep ☐
disturb ☐
injure ☐
break ▬
wait ☐

1
road ☐
watch ☐
trail ☐
lane ☐
cycle ☐

2
leaflet ☐
book ☐
organise ☐
read ☐
visit ☐

3
shape ☐
calculate ☐
toe ☐
hand ☐
digit ☐

4
bag ☐
box ☐
show ☐
case ☐
explain ☐

5
catch ☐
grab ☐
take ☐
barb ☐
snatch ☐

6
generous ☐
gift ☐
sell ☐
charity ☐
help ☐

7
calm ☐
balanced ☐
same ☐
soft ☐
even ☐

8
hold ☐
tanker ☐
vessel ☐
ferry ☐
sail ☐

9
jot ☐
letter ☐
part ☐
tear ☐
paper ☐

10
grasp ☐
palace ☐
tower ☐
keep ☐
secure ☐

How Did You Do? Let's Find Out!

Remember, there is no self-marking in this book. Please get an adult to mark your answers.

If you scored 7 or more out of 10

I consider these questions quite tricky so this is a good score but do look at the questions you got wrong so you understand how to score higher next time.

If you scored fewer than 7 out of 10

⇨ Look at the answers. You should be able to work out which words can have more than one meaning. If you can't then you should spend more time reading to help improve your vocabulary. Use the vocabulary builder on page 121 to write down any new words you come across and learn what they mean.

⇨ Remember to ask an adult to re-read the instructions and go through the example with you again if you didn't understand the questions. Then take another look at you answers and see if you can correct them. Remember you must choose a word which can be used instead of <u>all</u> of the words in the brackets.

LESSON 8 PART 2

My Time My Score

Now look at the questions below. Try to do each one as quickly as you can but make sure you finish them all. When you think you have found the right word mark it on the opposite page. You have six minutes to complete this task, so work quickly.

When you have finished write your time and score in the boxes above.

1 (post, letters) (armour, chain)
metal   pillar   mail   package   shield

2 (carton, parcel) (fill, load)
container   pack   wrap   store   bottle

3 (portray, show) (sketch, drawing)
picture   painting   shade   pencil   demonstrate

4 (mention, suggest) (lift, hoist)
offer   push   carry   raise   speak

5 (travel, journey) (span, area)
voyage   measure   cross   distance   range

6 (bag, pack) (plunder, loot)
shoulder   sack   suitcase   steal   snatch

7 (locked, sealed) (shield, guard)
key   vault   bank   secure   safe

8 (display, parade) (explain, instruct)
show   arrange   window   tell   understand

9 (extra, reserve) (free, unused)
more   above   derelict   share   spare

10 (pill, capsule) (slab, stone)
medicine   rock   tablet   ill   small

LESSON 8 PART 2: ANSWER SHEET

Mark your answer by putting a horizontal line in one of the boxes, as in the example below.

Example:

```
sleep   ☐
disturb ☐
injure  ☐
break   ▬
wait    ☐
```

1
```
metal    ☐
pillar   ☐
mail     ☐
package  ☐
shield   ☐
```

2
```
container ☐
pack      ☐
wrap      ☐
store     ☐
bottle    ☐
```

3
```
picture     ☐
painting    ☐
shade       ☐
pencil      ☐
demonstrate ☐
```

4
```
offer  ☐
push   ☐
carry  ☐
raise  ☐
speak  ☐
```

5
```
voyage   ☐
measure  ☐
cross    ☐
distance ☐
range    ☐
```

6
```
shoulder ☐
sack     ☐
suitcase ☐
steal    ☐
snatch   ☐
```

7
```
key    ☐
vault  ☐
bank   ☐
secure ☐
safe   ☐
```

8
```
show       ☐
arrange    ☐
window     ☐
tell       ☐
understand ☐
```

9
```
more     ☐
above    ☐
derelict ☐
share    ☐
spare    ☐
```

10
```
medicine ☐
rock     ☐
tablet   ☐
ill      ☐
small    ☐
```

LESSON 9 Working Out the Missing Letters for Each Sequence

In this exercise, you'll use the alphabet to help work out the missing letters that complete each sequence.

Remember, if you find that you get to the end of the alphabet but still need to make more jumps, just go back to the beginning and continue to count along the letters. Let's look at an example.

A B C D E F G H I J K L M N O P Q R S T U V W X Y Z

Example 1

C　　F　　I　　L　　_

In the example above there are two letters between each letter given or three 'jumps' to reach each. So the answer is <u>O</u>.

Example 2

TS　　UR　　VQ　　WP　　_

Here look at the first letter of each pair. You can see the pattern goes T, U, V, W so the next letter will be X as this is the next one along in the alphabet.

Then look at the second letter of each pair. Here the pattern goes S, R, Q, P moving back through the alphabet one letter each time. This means the next letter should be 'O'.

Your final answer then would be <u>XO</u> and that is what you would mark on your answer grid.

TIP FOR SPEEDING UP

Once again, looking straight at your answer sheet can help you. There are only five answer choices – try each one in turn to see if it fits the pattern or sequence.

LESSON 9 PRACTICE TEST

My Time

My Score

Now look at the questions below. Use the alphabet at the top of the list of questions to help you. When you've finished write down the time you took in the box above. Remember to get an adult to mark your answers and write down your score in the box at the top of this page too.

You have six minutes to complete this task, so work quickly.

The blank lines at the end of each series simply show you the position of the letters that are missing. You must mark your final answer on the corresponding grid on the opposite page.

A B C D E F G H I J K L M N O P Q R S T U V W X Y Z

1	A	B	E	J	_____
2	N	L	J	H	_____
3	R	S	Q	T	_____
4	P	L	I	G	_____
5	Y	B	W	D	_____
6	Q	N	K	H	_____
7	J	L	K	M	_____
8	J	I	L	K	_____
9	FE	IH	LK	ON	_____
10	CDE	HIJ	MNO	RST	_____

LESSON 9 PRACTICE TEST: ANSWER SHEET

Mark your answer by putting a horizontal line in one of the boxes, as in the examples below.

Example 1:

```
M ☐
N ☐
O ▬
P ☐
Q ☐
```

Example 2:

```
XT ☐
TX ☐
OX ☐
XO ▬
YO ☐
```

1
```
O ☐
P ☐
Q ☐
R ☐
S ☐
```

2
```
G ☐
F ☐
E ☐
D ☐
C ☐
```

3
```
P ☐
U ☐
V ☐
O ☐
S ☐
```

4
```
B ☐
C ☐
D ☐
E ☐
F ☐
```

5
```
V ☐
U ☐
E ☐
F ☐
T ☐
```

6
```
F ☐
E ☐
D ☐
G ☐
C ☐
```

7
```
L ☐
M ☐
N ☐
O ☐
P ☐
```

8
```
M ☐
N ☐
L ☐
O ☐
P ☐
```

9
```
PO ☐
QP ☐
RQ ☐
SR ☐
TS ☐
```

10
```
TUV ☐
UVW ☐
VWX ☐
WXY ☐
XYZ ☐
```

How Did You Do? Let's Find Out!

Remember, there is no self-marking in this book. Please get an adult to mark your answers.

If you scored between 8 and 10

A great score, well done! But do check over any questions you answered incorrectly to help you avoid these mistakes next time.

If you scored fewer than 8 out of 10

Remember to take care and use the alphabet provided at the top of the page – it's there to help you!

LESSON 10 Solving Problems with Information

This is another question type you haven't worked on before, so I have added more questions here for extra practice.

In this lesson you are asked to answer questions which relates to some information you have been given. These questions can take on a variety of forms.

Let's look at an example.

Example

The station clock is 9 minutes fast and the train which should have arrived at 3.12pm is 6 minutes late. What time does the clock show when the train arrives?

To answer this question first you add 6 minutes to 3.12pm to find out when the train arrived. This is 3.18pm.

This isn't the final answer though as you have also been told the station clock is 9 minutes fast. So you add 9 minutes to 3.18 pm and get the answer 3.27pm.

TIP FOR SPEEDING UP

- Find a starting point and work through the other information from there. If you're still struggling check with the answer grid and try to eliminate any obviously incorrect answers. This should help.

- If you notice that there are multiple questions about the same piece of information, it may be quicker to draw a simple table and enter the information – this way you'll be able to read it and answer the questions more quickly.

- For questions involving the order of several items based on weight, height or length, it may be helpful to draw a quick diagram showing the relationship between them all – this will also make information easier to read and use to answer questions.

LESSON 10 PART 1

My Time

My Score

Now look at the questions below. Try to do each one as quickly as you can but make sure you finish them all. Mark your answers on the opposite page. You have six minutes to complete this task, so work quickly. When you have finished write your time and score in the boxes above.

Kasim and Neil have 39 stickers between them; Neil and Carla have 44 stickers and the three children have a total of 65 stickers. Now answer the following questions.

1 How many stickers does Kasim have?

2 How many stickers does Carla have?

3 How many stickers do Carla and Kassim have between them?

Two years ago I was 15 and my father was 3 times my age.

4 How old will I be next year?

5 How old is my father now?

6 How old will I be when my father is twice my age?

Five children list the places they have visited. Dave and Gurpreet have been to Chester whilst Faiza and Carlton have been to Billericay. Dave, Gurpreet and Hamish have all been to Harrogate but only Carlton has been to Plaistow. Dave, Faiza and Carlton have been to Tadworth.

7 How many children have been to Harrogate?

8 How many children have been to three towns?

9 Who has been to Plaistow and Tadworth?

10 Who has visited only one town?

LESSON 10 PART 1: ANSWER SHEET

Mark your answer by putting a horizontal line in one of the boxes, as in the example below.

Example:

```
3.15pm ☐
3.17pm ☐
3.25pm ☐
3.27pm ▬
3.30pm ☐
```

1
- 18 ☐
- 19 ☐
- 20 ☐
- 21 ☐
- 22 ☐

2
- 18 ☐
- 21 ☐
- 26 ☐
- 39 ☐
- 44 ☐

3
- 26 ☐
- 39 ☐
- 44 ☐
- 47 ☐
- 65 ☐

4
- 15 ☐
- 16 ☐
- 17 ☐
- 18 ☐
- 19 ☐

5
- 41 ☐
- 43 ☐
- 45 ☐
- 47 ☐
- 49 ☐

6
- 20 ☐
- 25 ☐
- 30 ☐
- 35 ☐
- 40 ☐

7
- 1 ☐
- 2 ☐
- 3 ☐
- 4 ☐
- 5 ☐

8
- 1 ☐
- 2 ☐
- 3 ☐
- 4 ☐
- 5 ☐

9
- Dave ☐
- Gurpreet ☐
- Faiza ☐
- Carlton ☐
- Hamish ☐

10
- Dave ☐
- Gurpreet ☐
- Faiza ☐
- Carlton ☐
- Hamish ☐

How Did You Do? Let's Find Out!

Remember, there is no self-marking in this book. Please get an adult to mark your answers.

If you scored 7 or more out of 10

I consider these questions quite tricky (especially as they take so many different forms) so this is a good score but do look at the questions you got wrong to help you improve and try to score higher next time.

If you scored fewer than 7 out of 10

⇨ Go through your incorrect answers and work out where you went wrong. Try the different methods of drawing simple diagrams, tables and lists to help you improve at solving each type of question.

For example, to help you answer questions 7 to 10 you could draw a table like this:

	Places they have visited				
	CHESTER	**BILLERICAY**	**HARROGATE**	**PLAISTOW**	**TADWORTH**
Dave	✔		✔		✔
Gurpreet	✔		✔		
Faiza		✔			✔
Carlton		✔		✔	✔
Hamish			✔		

LESSON 10 PART 2

My Time

My Score

Now look at the questions below. Try to do each one as quickly as you can but make sure you finish them all. When you think you have found the answer mark it on the answer sheet opposite. You have six minutes to complete this task so work quickly.

When you have finished write your time and score in the boxes above.

Karl and Thelma have 37 books between them; Karl and Bruce have 31 books between them. The three children have 51 books in total.

1 How many books has Karl?

2 How many books does Thelma have?

3 How many books has Bruce?

4 How many books does Thelma have to give Bruce for all three children to have the same number?

Five children sit on chairs in a straight line. Barnaby is on the second chair from the left and Cecil sits next to him on his right. 2 chairs to the right of Barnaby sits Abigail who has Dion sitting on her right. Fred sits next to Barnaby.

5 Who sits in the middle of the row?

6 How many children sit between Dion and Fred?

7 Who sits on the left of Abigail?

8 Who sits either side of Barnaby?

9 If Abigail swaps places with Fred, who now sits on her right?

10 If my watch is 3 minutes slow and my television programme starts 8 minutes later than its 11.20am scheduled time, what time does my watch show when the programme begins?

LESSON 10 PART 2: ANSWER SHEET

Mark your answer by putting a horizontal line in one of the boxes, as in the example below.

Example:

| 3.15pm ☐ |
| 3.17pm ☐ |
| 3.25pm ☐ |
| 3.27pm ▬ |
| 3.30pm ☐ |

1
- 14 ☐
- 17 ☐
- 31 ☐
- 37 ☐
- 51 ☐

2
- 14 ☐
- 17 ☐
- 20 ☐
- 31 ☐
- 37 ☐

3
- 14 ☐
- 17 ☐
- 20 ☐
- 31 ☐
- 37 ☐

4
- 1 ☐
- 2 ☐
- 3 ☐
- 4 ☐
- 5 ☐

5
- Fred ☐
- Abigail ☐
- Dion ☐
- Cecil ☐
- Nobody ☐

6
- 0 ☐
- 1 ☐
- 2 ☐
- 3 ☐
- 4 ☐

7
- Fred ☐
- Dion ☐
- Cecil ☐
- Barnaby ☐
- Nobody ☐

8
- Fred/Dion ☐
- Dion/Abigail ☐
- Cecil/Abigail ☐
- Dion/Cecil ☐
- Fred/Cecil ☐

9
- Fred ☐
- Barnaby ☐
- Dion ☐
- Cecil ☐
- Nobody ☐

10
- 11.25 am ☐
- 11.27 am ☐
- 11.29 am ☐
- 11.31 am ☐
- 11.33 am ☐

LESSON 11 Working Out Indirect Codes for Words

In this exercise, you're given one word and told the code for it. You'll then need to apply the same code to another word. Each question will have a different code.

These questions can have different forms. Look at the three examples below which illustrate this.

A B C D E F G H I J K L M N O P Q R S T U V W X Y Z

1 The word and code have the same number of letters:

Example 1

If TRAIN is written SSZJM, how do you write STEAM?

In this case, by looking at the alphabet, you can see that S is one jump back from T, the second S is one jump forward from R, Z is one jump back from A, J is one jump forward from I and M is one jump back from N. If you apply this code to STEAM it is written <u>RUDBL</u>.

2 Sometimes a word might be written backwards:

Example 2

If TOOL is written LOOT, how do you write REED?

As TOOL is written in reverse to make LOOT, REED is written as <u>DEER</u>.

3 Sometimes numbers are used. Often these refer to the corresponding letter of the alphabet, for example A = 1, B = 2, but not always so watch out for these.

Example 3

If COMB is written 3 P 13 C, how do you write HAIR?

In this case numbers have been used for two of the letters and you can see that the other two letters have simply moved on one jump forward in the alphabet. So HAIR is written <u>8 B 9 S</u>.

TIPS FOR SPEEDING UP

- These questions can take quite some time to work out, so try being crafty and use the multiple choice answer sheet to help you.

- First figure out what the code is using one of the methods you saw in the examples on page 56. Then look at the answer choices. You might find that two of the answers in the grid begin with the same letter. Now work out the first letter of the answer. If you work out the first letter correctly, you can eliminate several of the answers very quickly.

- If you notice that all the answers in the grid begin with the same letter, don't even bother to work it out! 'Why not?' I hear you shout! Because if they all begin with the same letter that must be correct so you don't need to work it out. Instead look at the last letter and see if there are any differences there – again this will really help you motor through!

LESSON 11 PRACTICE TEST

My Time

My Score

Now look at the questions below. Try to do them as quickly as possible and mark your answer on the answer sheet opposite. Move on if you find any particular question tricky, you can always come back to it. When you've finished write down the time you took in the box above. Remember to get an adult to mark your answers. Then write down your score in the box at the top of this page.

You have six minutes to complete this task, so work quickly.

A B C D E F G H I J K L M N O P Q R S T U V W X Y Z

1. If FOOT is written as ENNS, how would you write HAND?

2. If PMAI means ROCK, what does QYLB mean?

3. If SOIL is written as TQLP, how would you write DIRT?

4. If VNOMV means ARROW, what does KKFLS mean?

5. If DOOR is written as DEOFOGRH, what does WEAFLGLH mean?

6. If MOOR is written as ROOM, how would you write STUN?

7. If RIP means TIP, what does LIP mean?

8. If FOLD is written as EPKE, what does VSZQ mean?

9. If 20 1 11 5 means TAKE, what does 7 9 22 5 mean?

10. If BEND is written as 2 G 14 F, how would you write CURL?

LESSON 11 PRACTICE TEST: ANSWER SHEET

Mark your answer by putting a horizontal line in one of the boxes, as in the examples below.

Example 1:

RTDBL	☐
RUCBL	☐
RTDCL	☐
RUDCL	☐
RUDBL	▬

Example 2:

DARE	☐
RAID	☐
DEAR	☐
DEER	▬
LOOT	☐

Example 3:

9 B 8 S	☐
8 B 9 S	▬
8 B 9 T	☐
9 C 9 S	☐
8 B 9 T	☐

1

HZMC	☐
GZMC	☐
IZMC	☐
GZMD	☐
GZME	☐

2

BAND	☐
WAND	☐
SAND	☐
SANG	☐
LANE	☐

3

DKUX	☐
ELUX	☐
DLUY	☐
ELUY	☐
EKUX	☐

4

PAINT	☐
POINT	☐
PAINS	☐
JOINT	☐
SAINT	☐

5

WAIL	☐
WILL	☐
WELL	☐
WALL	☐
WALK	☐

6

TUNS	☐
NUTS	☐
NETS	☐
TENS	☐
NEST	☐

7

RIP	☐
PIP	☐
SIP	☐
NIP	☐
DIP	☐

8

WEEP	☐
WRAP	☐
WARN	☐
WARE	☐
TRAP	☐

9

HIVE	☐
DIVE	☐
GIVE	☐
LIVE	☐
GAME	☐

10

2 W 18 N	☐
3 W 17 N	☐
3 W 18 M	☐
2 W 18 M	☐
3 W 18 N	☐

How Did You Do? Let's Find Out!

Remember, there is no self-marking in this book. Please get an adult to mark your answers.

If you scored between 7 and 10

Great work! But do check over any questions you got wrong to help you avoid these mistakes next time.

If you scored fewer than 7 out of 10

⇨ Remember you need to figure out the codes carefully by checking letters or numbers or looking to see if one word is placed inside another.

⇨ Do you understand what you have to do? If not, ask an adult to read the instructions and go through the examples with you again.

⇨ Writing neatly and tidily will help you avoid unnecessary mistakes in your working. Make sure you are careful when filling in your answer on the grid as well.

LESSON 12 Completing Number Patterns

In this exercise you'll need to look at a list of numbers and work out what the pattern is. Then you'll need to decide which number should come next.

Let's look at some examples.

Example 1

      5   9   13   17   ____

In this example you can see that the numbers increase by 4 each time so the next number must be 21.

Example 2

    14   7   9   12   4   ____

In this example you'll need to skip a number each time as there are two different patterns. The first pattern goes from 14 to 9 to 4 decreasing by 5 each time. The second pattern goes from 7 to 12 to 17 increasing by 5 each time. So 17 will be your answer.

Example 3

    209   328   447   566   ____

In this example you'll need to look at each digit individually. You can see that the first digit of each number increases by one each time, the second increases by two each time and the third decreases by one each time. So your answer should be 685.

TIP FOR SPEEDING UP

Once you think you know what the pattern or sequence is look at the answer sheet and see which of the answers fits the sequence.

LESSON 12 PRACTICE TEST

My Time   My Score

Now look at the questions below. Work out which number should come next in each pattern. Remember to mark your answer on the opposite page – don't write it on the blank line. When you've finished write down the time you took in the box above. Get an adult to mark your answers then write down your score in the box at the top of this page too.

Work quickly – you have six minutes to complete this task.

#						
1	6	7	13	14	20	_____
2	9	18	27	36	45	_____
3	3	4	7	11	18	_____
4	81	64	49	36	25	_____
5	2	6	18	54	162	_____
6	5	3	8	6	11	_____
7	82	28	73	37	64	_____
8	387	486	585	684	783	_____
9	2.34	2.46	2.58	2.70	2.82	_____
10	16	8	24	12	36	_____

LESSON 12 PRACTICE TEST: ANSWER SHEET

Mark your answer by putting a horizontal line in one of the boxes, as in the examples below.

Example 1:

- 18 ☐
- 19 ☐
- 20 ☐
- 21 ▬
- 22 ☐

Example 2:

- −1 ☐
- 15 ☐
- 16 ☐
- 17 ▬
- 4 ☐

Example 3:

- 677 ☐
- 675 ☐
- 875 ☐
- 687 ☐
- 685 ▬

1
- 21 ☐
- 22 ☐
- 23 ☐
- 24 ☐
- 25 ☐

2
- 54 ☐
- 56 ☐
- 58 ☐
- 60 ☐
- 62 ☐

3
- 27 ☐
- 28 ☐
- 29 ☐
- 30 ☐
- 31 ☐

4
- 14 ☐
- 15 ☐
- 16 ☐
- 17 ☐
- 18 ☐

5
- 386 ☐
- 165 ☐
- 286 ☐
- 186 ☐
- 486 ☐

6
- 9 ☐
- 11 ☐
- 13 ☐
- 15 ☐
- 17 ☐

7
- 28 ☐
- 37 ☐
- 73 ☐
- 82 ☐
- 46 ☐

8
- 882 ☐
- 883 ☐
- 884 ☐
- 885 ☐
- 886 ☐

9
- 2.84 ☐
- 2.86 ☐
- 2.88 ☐
- 2.92 ☐
- 2.94 ☐

10
- 48 ☐
- 14 ☐
- 16 ☐
- 18 ☐
- 54 ☐

How Did You Do? Let's Find Out!

Remember, there is no self-marking in this book. Please get an adult to mark your answers.

If you scored between 8 and 10

Well done, this is a good score! But do check over any questions you got wrong to help you improve your score next time.

If you scored fewer than 8 out of 10

⇨ Learn your multiplication facts (some people might call these times tables) off by heart as this will help you speed up on these numbers.

⇨ If you don't understand the question, ask an adult to read the instructions and go through the examples with you again.

⇨ Work out the pattern by using your knowledge of addition, subtraction, multiplication and division.

⇨ Look out for questions which have two different patterns and those for which you have to look at each digit individually.

⇨ Make sure you can recognise set patterns such as prime, square and cube numbers. If you need help with these go back to lesson 12 in the first book in the series, *Discover Verbal Reasoning*.

LESSON 13 Calculating Number Sentences

A number sentence is also known as an 'equation'. Usually you'll be given a set of calculations and will be told that the answer should be equal to that of a second set of calculations. You often have to find a missing number to make the sentence complete and correct.

This is another question type that you haven't worked on before, so I have included two sets of questions here for extra practice.

In these questions you need to identify the missing number (without using a calculator!). To do this, you need to look at both sides of the equation and work out both sums. Start with the side which has all of its numbers. Then work out which number will make the sum on the other side of the equation equal to this amount.

Example

$$4 \times 3 + 8 = (2 + 2) \times \underline{}$$

The answer to the example above should be $\underline{5}$ since $4 \times 3 = 12$ then $+ 8 = 20$.

So $2 + 2 = 4$ and must be multiplied by $\underline{5}$ to make the same amount.

TIPS FOR SPEEDING UP

- For these questions you should always work out the side which has all the numbers first. Additionally you should write its final amount just above the numbers on your question paper. This will help you when you look at the other part of the equation so you don't have to hold too many numbers in your head.

- If you get stuck then use the answers from the multiple choice grid and try each one in turn – that way you should be able to work out the answer even if it's tough.

LESSON 13 PART 1

My Time

My Score

Now look at the questions below. When you think you have found the missing number mark it on the opposite page. You have six minutes to complete this task, so work quickly.

When you have finished write your time and score in the boxes above.

1 (13 + 7) ÷ 2 = 56 ÷ 7 + _____

2 9 × 12 − 20 = (15 − 7) × _____

3 42 ÷ 6 + 23 = 300 ÷ 2 ÷ _____

4 (19 + 17) ÷ 4 = (100 − 19) ÷ _____

5 (15 + 2) × 5 = 23 × 4 − _____

6 72 ÷ _____ = 40 ÷ 8 + 1

7 (43 − 17) × _____ = (12 × 11) − 28

8 _____ ÷ 4 = 9 × 2 − 5

9 (37 − 20) × _____ = 11 × 6 − 15

10 5 × 15 − _____ = 14 × 3 + 8

LESSON 13 PART 1: ANSWER SHEET

Mark your answer by putting a horizontal line in one of the boxes, as in the example below.

Example:

```
 4 ☐
 5 ▬
 6 ☐
10 ☐
12 ☐
```

1
```
1 ☐
2 ☐
3 ☐
4 ☐
5 ☐
```

2
```
 8 ☐
 9 ☐
10 ☐
11 ☐
12 ☐
```

3
```
1 ☐
2 ☐
3 ☐
4 ☐
5 ☐
```

4
```
 7 ☐
 8 ☐
 9 ☐
10 ☐
11 ☐
```

5
```
5 ☐
6 ☐
7 ☐
8 ☐
9 ☐
```

6
```
12 ☐
13 ☐
14 ☐
15 ☐
16 ☐
```

7
```
1 ☐
2 ☐
3 ☐
4 ☐
5 ☐
```

8
```
50 ☐
51 ☐
52 ☐
53 ☐
54 ☐
```

9
```
0 ☐
1 ☐
2 ☐
3 ☐
4 ☐
```

10
```
 5 ☐
10 ☐
15 ☐
20 ☐
25 ☐
```

How Did You Do? Let's Find Out!

Remember, there is no self-marking in this book. Please get an adult to mark your answers.

If you scored 8 or more out of 10

Great work but do look at the questions you got wrong to help you understand where you made mistakes.

If you scored fewer than 8 out of 10

⇨ Make sure you know your multiplication facts thoroughly and that you can subtract and add numbers quickly to help you with these.

⇨ Do you understand what you have to do? If not, ask an adult to re-read the instructions and go through the example with you again. Then take another look at your answers and see if you can correct them.

⇨ Remember that each calculation on either side of the 'equals' sign needs to have the same total.

LESSON 13 PART 2

My Time   My Score

Now look at the questions below. Try to do each one as quickly as you can and make sure you finish them all. When you think you have found the missing number mark it on the opposite page. You have six minutes to complete this task, so work quickly.

When you have finished write your time and score in the boxes above.

1 23 − (2 × 9)   =   (12 + 3) ÷ _____

2 11 × _____ + 29   =   50 × (15 ÷ 5)

3 4 × 15 − 7   =   28 × _____ − 3

4 2.5 × 8   =   _____ × 2 − 4

5 (7 + 4) × _____   =   (27 − 5) × 3

6 (18 − 9) × (3 × 3) = 10 × 10 − (_____ + 6)

7 (6 × 7) × _____   =   (3 + 4) × 12

8 14 ÷ 2 + _____   =   (10 ÷ 2) × 5

9 17 × 4 − 14   =   (_____ + 2) × 9

10 57 − 9 ÷ _____   =   (32 − 16) ÷ 2

LESSON 13 PART 2: ANSWER SHEET

Mark your answer by putting a horizontal line in one of the boxes, as in the example below.

Example:

```
 4 ☐
 5 ▬
 6 ☐
10 ☐
12 ☐
```

1
```
1 ☐
2 ☐
3 ☐
4 ☐
5 ☐
```

2
```
 8 ☐
 9 ☐
10 ☐
11 ☐
12 ☐
```

3
```
1 ☐
2 ☐
3 ☐
4 ☐
5 ☐
```

4
```
 8 ☐
 9 ☐
10 ☐
11 ☐
12 ☐
```

5
```
5 ☐
6 ☐
7 ☐
8 ☐
9 ☐
```

6
```
12 ☐
13 ☐
14 ☐
15 ☐
16 ☐
```

7
```
1 ☐
2 ☐
3 ☐
4 ☐
5 ☐
```

8
```
15 ☐
16 ☐
17 ☐
18 ☐
19 ☐
```

9
```
0 ☐
1 ☐
2 ☐
3 ☐
4 ☐
```

10
```
5 ☐
6 ☐
7 ☐
8 ☐
9 ☐
```

LESSON 14 Solving Coded Analogies

In this exercise you're given one or two letters and shown how these are turned into a code. You'll then use this information to work out the code for the second set of letters. The key point to remember here is that the two sets of letters should always be turned into codes in the same way. Let's look at some examples.

A B C D E F G H I J K L M N O P Q R S T U V W X Y Z

Example 1

D is to F as   G is to ?

Using the alphabet you can see that to get from D to F you need to take two 'jumps' forward so you must also make this number of jumps from the letter G to find your answer. If you do this you can see that your answer is I.

Example 2

CA is to FD as   PN is to ?

In this example there are pairs of letters but you should begin by looking at each letter individually. If you count from C to F you can see that this is three 'jumps' so you must apply this code to the letter P. This gives you S as the first letter to your answer.

Then you look at the number of 'jumps' from A to D and you see that this is also three so you must do the same again with the letter N. So the second letter in your answer will be Q.

So your final answer is SQ and you should mark this on your answer grid.

TIPS FOR SPEEDING UP

- It's difficult to do these questions quickly. The best thing to do is to work out the code for the first letters, then work out your answer and then look at the multiple choice answer sheet.

- If your answer is there, that's great, if it isn't check which answer choice is closest in the alphabet to your answer. Go back to the question to double-check this letter is the correct one.

LESSON 14 PRACTICE TEST

My Time

My Score

Now look at the questions below and try to work them out as quickly as you can. Use the alphabet at the top of the list of questions to help you.

When you've finished write down the time you took in the box above. Remember to get an adult to mark your answers. Then write down your score in the box at the top of this page.

You have six minutes to complete this task.

A B C D E F G H I J K L M N O P Q R S T U V W X Y Z

1. C is to X   as   F is to

2. L is to J   as   R is to

3. F is to I   as   T is to

4. M is to H   as   C is to

5. W is to B   as   J is to

6. TS is to WV   as   HG is to

7. PR is to UW   as   BD is to

8. LO is to NQ   as   WZ is to

9. DB is to ZX   as   VT is to

10. JQ is to KP   as   LO is to

LESSON 14 PRACTICE TEST: ANSWER SHEET

Mark your answer by putting a horizontal line in one of the boxes, as in the examples below.

Example 1:

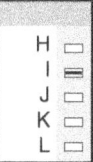

Example 2:

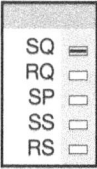

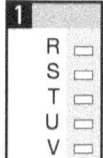

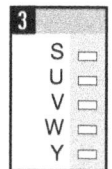
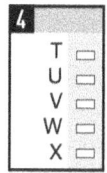

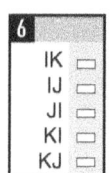
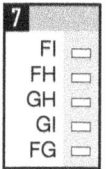

How Did You Do? Let's Find Out!

Remember, there is no self-marking in this book. Please get an adult to mark your answers.

If you scored between 8 and 10

This is a great score! Remember to check over any questions you got wrong and make sure you understand why you made those mistakes.

If you scored fewer than 8 out of 10

⇨ Don't lose valuable time by spending too much time on one question if it's causing problems, move on to the others and go back to it.

⇨ Make sure you count the differences between letters correctly. It's easy to make a mistake while doing this so be careful. Use the alphabet given to you to help with this.

⇨ Do you understand what you have to do? If not, ask an adult to read the instructions and go through the examples with you again.

⇨ Make sure you work out the first part of the code by looking at the first set of letters and then apply the same code to the second set.

LESSON 15 Finding Analogical Words

In this exercise you're given two groups of three words. You'll need to choose the two words that relate to the prompt words <u>in the same way</u>. If that sounds tricky don't worry, the following example will help you understand.

Example

        tasty is to   (sour   food   flavoursome)
        as calm is to   (restless   tranquil   storm)

In this example you start by looking how the word 'tasty' relates to the words in its group and you can see that...

1. Sour has a completely different meaning to tasty
2. Food is something that could be tasty
3. Flavoursome is a synonym of tasty (it has a similar meaning)

Then you look at the second set of words and you see how the word 'calm' relates to these:

1. Restless is the antonym of calm (it is its opposite)
2. Tranquil is a synonym of calm
3. Storm is something which is not calm

If you compare both sets of words you can see that <u>flavoursome</u> and <u>tranquil</u> are the correct answers since these are both words that are synonyms of the words outside the brackets. You would mark both of these on your answer grid.

TIPS FOR SPEEDING UP

- These may be difficult to do quickly if you don't have a good understanding of word meanings and vocabulary. The best thing to do is to broaden your vocabulary by reading regularly and making a list of any new words you come across and how they are used on the vocabulary builder on page 121.

- If you get stuck on a question, don't waste time on it – move on and return to it if you have time.

LESSON 15 PRACTICE TEST

My Time   My Score

Now look at the questions below and try to work them out as quickly as you can. Remember to mark two answers on your answer grid – one word from each set of brackets. When you've finished write down the time you took in the box above. Get an adult to mark your answers. Then write down your score in the box at the top of this page.

You have six minutes to complete this task, so work quickly.

1	drink is to as read is to	(swallow (book	liquid write	bottle) pencil)
2	camera is to as toaster is to	(digital (bread	colour toast	photograph) crumbs)
3	dog is to as snake is to	(fur (poison	bite hiss	bark) slither)
4	day is to as month is to	(light (thirty	time long	week) year)
5	mile is to as gram is to	(walk (volume	distance weight	long) measure)
6	library is to as butcher is to	(books (chop	quiet meet	town) meat)
7	port is to as station is to	(place (police	ship paper	bus) train)
8	pots is to as step is to	(crash (see	stop talk	noise) pets)
9	cunning is to as strong is to	(slow (muscles	fox big	think) ox)
10	high is to as narrow is to	(low (broad	tall street	huge) passage)

LESSON 15 PRACTICE TEST: ANSWER SHEET

Mark your answer by putting a horizontal line in one of the boxes for each set of words as in the example below.

Example:

sour ☐	restless ☐
food ☐	tranquil ▬
flavoursome ▬	storm ☐

1

swallow ☐	book ☐
liquid ☐	write ☐
bottle ☐	pencil ☐

2

digital ☐	bread ☐
colour ☐	toast ☐
photograph ☐	crumbs ☐

3

fur ☐	poison ☐
bite ☐	hiss ☐
bark ☐	slither ☐

4

light ☐	thirty ☐
time ☐	long ☐
week ☐	year ☐

5

walk ☐	volume ☐
distance ☐	weight ☐
long ☐	measure ☐

6

books ☐	chop ☐
quiet ☐	meet ☐
town ☐	meat ☐

7

place ☐	police ☐
ship ☐	paper ☐
bus ☐	train ☐

8

crash ☐	see ☐
stop ☐	talk ☐
noise ☐	pets ☐

9

slow ☐	muscles ☐
fox ☐	big ☐
think ☐	ox ☐

10

low ☐	broad ☐
tall ☐	street ☐
huge ☐	passage ☐

How Did You Do? Let's Find Out!

Remember, there is no self-marking in this book. Please get an adult to mark your answers.

If you scored between 8 and 10

Well done, this is a great score! Make sure you understand where you made mistakes though.

If you scored fewer than 8 out of 10

⇨ Don't lose valuable time by spending too much time on one particular question if it's causing problems, move on and come back to it later.

⇨ Do you understand what you have to do? If not, ask an adult to read the instructions and go through the example with you again.

⇨ Remember to work out the relationship between both sets of words and mark two words on your answer grid.

LESSON 16 Finding the Two Words Which Don't Belong in the Group

The rest of the lessons in this book feature question types that you haven't worked on before, so I have added two sets of questions in each for extra practice.

In this exercise, three of the five words in each group belong together. Two of the words don't. You need to find these two words and mark them on the answer sheet. Let's look at an example.

Example

      red   brown   colour   shade   azure

In this example the two words that don't belong to the group are <u>colour</u> and <u>shade</u> because all the other words are colours.

Colour itself does not belong in the group as it isn't itself a colour.

Shade isn't a type of colour even though one may be tricked into choosing it – don't!

Azure is a colour and you should add this word to the vocabulary builder on page 121 if you didn't know it.

HELPFUL HINTS

- If the words you are given are difficult you could use the process of elimination to find your answers.

- First identify what the theme of the group is and which three words go together.

- If you aren't sure what a word means, skip over it and try to work out whether the others belong together first.

- Beware of 'generic' words.

  Generic words describe the group of words but don't actually belong in the group themselves.

  'Colour' is a generic word in the example above, so although 'colour' describes the other words in the group, the word itself isn't actually a colour so it doesn't belong.

LESSON 16 PART 1

My Time

My Score

Now look at the questions below. Try to do each one as quickly as you can and make sure you finish them all. Remember you must put a mark against <u>two</u> answers on the answer grid opposite for each question. When you've finished write down the time you took in the box above. Get an adult to mark your answers. Then write down your score in the box at the top of this page.

You have six minutes to complete this task, so work quickly.

1	gigantic	minute	far	colossal	mighty
2	tiny	hardy	beautiful	robust	healthy
3	invade	capture	conquer	retreat	negotiate
4	lazy	hurried	sluggish	sweaty	idle
5	servant	humble	master	lord	leader
6	wall	nook	crevice	field	hollow
7	peck	stroke	bite	listen	nip
8	pop	whisper	crack	bang	fly
9	marsh	cliff	mire	beach	bog
10	tile	seat	chair	bench	road

LESSON 16 PART 1: ANSWER SHEET

Mark your answers by putting two horizontal lines in each of the grids, as in the example below.

Example:

```
red    ☐
brown  ☐
colour ▬
shade  ▬
azure  ☐
```

1
```
gigantic ☐
minute   ☐
far      ☐
colossal ☐
mighty   ☐
```

2
```
tiny      ☐
hardy     ☐
beautiful ☐
robust    ☐
healthy   ☐
```

3
```
invade    ☐
capture   ☐
conquer   ☐
retreat   ☐
negotiate ☐
```

4
```
lazy     ☐
hurried  ☐
sluggish ☐
sweaty   ☐
idle     ☐
```

5
```
servant ☐
humble  ☐
master  ☐
lord    ☐
leader  ☐
```

6
```
wall    ☐
nook    ☐
crevice ☐
field   ☐
hollow  ☐
```

7
```
peck   ☐
stroke ☐
bite   ☐
listen ☐
nip    ☐
```

8
```
pop     ☐
whisper ☐
crack   ☐
bang    ☐
fly     ☐
```

9
```
marsh ☐
cliff ☐
mire  ☐
beach ☐
bog   ☐
```

10
```
tile  ☐
seat  ☐
chair ☐
bench ☐
road  ☐
```

How Did You Do? Let's Find Out!

Remember, there is no self-marking in this book. Please get an adult to mark your answers.

If you scored between 8 and 10

This is great! Move on to the next set and try to continue your good work. Do look at any questions you got wrong and learn any words that are new to you.

If you scored fewer than 8 out of 10

⇨ Do you understand what you have to do? If not, ask an adult to read the instructions and go through the example with you again. Then take another look at your answers and see if you can correct them. Remember you must find the two words which don't belong in the group.

⇨ Beware of words which can have more than one meaning – they can make the questions tricky. Make sure you consider all meanings when choosing your answer.

⇨ Try reading some more challenging books – and note down any new words and what they mean as you come across them.

LESSON 16 PART 2

My Time **My Score**

Now try the questions below. Remember you'll need to put a mark against two answers on your multiple choice grid. These are quite tough and I've even thrown in a number question of the same style to really test you! When you've finished write down the time you took in the box above. Get an adult to mark your answers, then write down your score in the box at the top of this page.

You only have six minutes to complete this task, so work quickly. If you do get stuck, move on and return to any tricky questions at the end.

1	fox	ocelot	panther	jaguar	bear
2	cylinder	rectangle	cone	sphere	triangle
3	lettuce	cucumber	pineapple	chicken	leek
4	barrel	chest	house	trunk	key
5	vest	clothes	shirt	blouse	wool
6	secure	open	tight	loose	fixed
7	reflex	obtuse	angle	acute	degrees
8	humid	cool	windy	cold	fresh
9	25	36	80	20	49
10	dirty	plain	spotless	grimy	filthy

LESSON 16 PART 2: ANSWER SHEET

Mark your answers by putting two horizontal lines in each of the grids, as in the example below.

Example:

```
red   ☐
brown ☐
colour ▰
shade  ▰
azure  ☐
```

1
```
fox    ☐
ocelot ☐
panther ☐
jaguar ☐
bear   ☐
```

2
```
cylinder  ☐
rectangle ☐
cone      ☐
sphere    ☐
triangle  ☐
```

3
```
lettuce   ☐
cucumber  ☐
pineapple ☐
chicken   ☐
leek      ☐
```

4
```
barrel ☐
chest  ☐
house  ☐
trunk  ☐
key    ☐
```

5
```
vest    ☐
clothes ☐
shirt   ☐
blouse  ☐
wool    ☐
```

6
```
secure ☐
open   ☐
tight  ☐
loose  ☐
fixed  ☐
```

7
```
reflex  ☐
obtuse  ☐
angle   ☐
acute   ☐
degrees ☐
```

8
```
humid ☐
cool  ☐
windy ☐
cold  ☐
fresh ☐
```

9
```
25 ☐
36 ☐
80 ☐
20 ☐
49 ☐
```

10
```
dirty    ☐
plain    ☐
spotless ☐
grimy    ☐
filthy   ☐
```

LESSON 17 Working Out the Missing Codes for Each Word

In this exercise, you're given five codes in number form. These codes match the five words which are also given. You'll need to find out which word goes with which code before you can answer the questions that follow.

Let's look at an example.

Example

The codes 5463, 6423, 5246, 6352 and 2463 represent the words REST, STIR, SIRE, TIRE and RITE but not in that order.

1 How would you write the code for TEST?

2 What does the code 526332 stand for?

So for question 1: TEST = <u>2352</u> and for question 2: 526332 = <u>STREET</u>

HELPFUL HINTS

- Look for similarities and differences between the words. For example, do any of the words start or end with a different letter from the others? If so you may well be able to work out several of the letters and the numbers that represent them quickly.

- Once you have worked out one of the codes for one of the words, write that code above that word. Then you can write the corresponding numbers for letters on the other words which should unlock codes for them. I show you how to do this below.

First you can see that only one word – TIRE – begins with a 'T'. Looking at the number codes you can see that two of then begin with a '5', two begin with a '6' and only one begins with a '2'. 2463 must therefore stand for TIRE.

So you now know that T = 2, I = 4, R = 6 and E = 3.

From this, you can work out the other words:

REST = 6352   STIR = 5246   SIRE = 5463   TIRE = 2463   RITE = 6423

Once you know this information you can then answer the questions.

LESSON 17 PART 1

My Time

My Score

Now look at the questions below. Complete as many questions as you can and mark your answers on the answer sheet. When you've finished write down the time you took in the box above. Remember to get an adult to mark your answers. Then write down your score in the box above too.

You have six minutes to work these out, so work quickly.

A The codes 7152, 7159, 9517, 5217 and 9215 represent the words TEAR, RATE, RATS, SEAT and STAR, but not necessarily in that order.

How do you write:

1 RATES

2 TEASE

3 STARES

What do these codes mean?

4 2195

5 57229

6 5295

B The numbers 4368, 6814, 8341, 1438 and 6381 represent the words TIME, SITE, STEM, EMIT and MIST, but not necessarily in that order.

How do you write:

7 ESTEEM

8 MEETS

9 SMITE

10 TIMES

LESSON 17 PART 1: ANSWER SHEET

Mark your answer by putting a horizontal line in one of the boxes, as in the examples below.

Example 1:

2235 ☐
2352 ▬
5323 ☐
5332 ☐
2325 ☐

Example 2:

TREATS ☐
TRIERS ☐
STEERS ☐
RESITS ☐
STREET ▬

1
71529 ☐
71528 ☐
61529 ☐
72529 ☐
72519 ☐

2
52193 ☐
53192 ☐
52292 ☐
52192 ☐
53292 ☐

3
851729 ☐
952729 ☐
951829 ☐
951739 ☐
951729 ☐

4
SEAT ☐
EATS ☐
EAST ☐
TEAS ☐
TEST ☐

5
TEARS ☐
STEER ☐
STARE ☐
TREES ☐
RATES ☐

6
SEAT ☐
TEST ☐
SETS ☐
EATS ☐
TEAS ☐

7
168224 ☐
268114 ☐
168114 ☐
178114 ☐
168115 ☐

8
42286 ☐
41196 ☐
41187 ☐
41188 ☐
41186 ☐

9
54381 ☐
64381 ☐
64382 ☐
54382 ☐
64391 ☐

10
83417 ☐
83516 ☐
83426 ☐
83418 ☐
83416 ☐

How Did You Do? Let's Find Out!

Remember, there is no self-marking in this book. Please get an adult to mark your answers.

If you scored between 8 and 10

This is great! Move on to the next set of questions and try to continue your good work. But do check over any questions you got wrong.

If you scored fewer than 8 out of 10

⇨ Make sure that you figure out the codes correctly <u>before</u> you work out the answers to each specific question. Test your codes to make sure they are correct.

⇨ Do you understand what you have to do? If not, ask an adult to read the instructions and go through the example with you again.

⇨ Make sure you work out the codes – some students simply write the words they are given above the numbers in order. But this <u>isn't</u> correct – the codes aren't always given in the same order as the words so you need to work them out each time.

LESSON 17 PART 2

My Time

My Score

Now it's time to try some more. Get an adult to mark your answers, then write down your score in the box at the top of this page next to the time you took.

You have six minutes for this task. Remember to mark your answers on the page opposite.

A 74251, 15436, 75231, 72561, 13456, represent: FLITS, FAILS, FILES, STALE, SLATE

What do these codes mean?

1 132756

2 76431

3 52731

4 13645

B The codes 1542, 2541, 3542, 1425 and 1435 represent the words TEAR, DEAR, DATE, READ and DARE but not necessarily in that order.

How do you write:

5 DREADED

6 DART

7 RATED

What do these codes mean?

8 32415

9 342

10 1541

LESSON 17 PART 2: ANSWER SHEET

Mark your answer by putting a horizontal line in one of the boxes, as in the examples below.

Example 1:

2235 ☐
2352 ▬
5323 ☐
5332 ☐
2325 ☐

Example 2:

TREATS ☐
TRIERS ☐
STEERS ☐
RESITS ☐
STREET ▬

1
TRIFLE ☐
RIFLES ☐
STIFLE ☐
FILTER ☐
STILTS ☐

2
STEAL ☐
FEATS ☐
FEAST ☐
FLEET ☐
STAIL ☐

3
TALES ☐
LEAST ☐
LASTS ☐
TASTE ☐
LIFTS ☐

4
SEATS ☐
STEAL ☐
SLEET ☐
SEALS ☐
STATE ☐

5
1254141 ☐
1255151 ☐
1245151 ☐
1254151 ☐
1255141 ☐

6
1234 ☐
4321 ☐
1423 ☐
1342 ☐
1243 ☐

7
24351 ☐
24531 ☐
24153 ☐
24315 ☐
24513 ☐

8
RADAR ☐
DATED ☐
RATED ☐
TRADE ☐
DREAD ☐

9
EAR ☐
RAT ☐
ARE ☐
ATE ☐
TAR ☐

10
DEAD ☐
READ ☐
TEAR ☐
RATE ☐
DARE ☐

LESSON 18 Completing the Third Pair of Words Using the Same Pattern

In this exercise, you'll need to look at the first two pairs of words to work out how the second word of each pair is formed. Then you'll use this information to work out the second word for the third pair. All three pairs should make the second word in the same way. Let's look at some examples.

Example 1

grant → rant   flame → lame   track → ?

In this example, the second word in each pair is formed by removing the first letter of the first word. If you remove the first letter of the given word in the third pair you can work out that the missing word would be <u>rack</u>.

Example 2

doom → mood   lever → revel   brag → ?

In this example, the second word in each pair is formed by simply reversing the first word. Therefore the second word in the third pair should be <u>brag</u> spelled backwards, which is <u>garb</u>.

Example 3

base → care   cast → dart   ruse → ?

In this example, two changes have occurred: (i) the first letter of each first word has jumped onwards by one in the alphabet; and (ii) the third letter of each first word has jumped back by one in the alphabet. The other letters remain the same.

If you apply this rule to the third pair of words, 'r' should become 's' and 's' should become 'r' giving you the word <u>sure</u> as the correct answer.

HELPFUL HINT

There are many different ways in which letters can be moved and words changed. So look really carefully and compare the first two pairs of words to see where changes have happened in both. Only then can you work out the third pair.

LESSON 18 PART 1

My Time

My Score

Now look at the questions below. Try to do each one as quickly as you can, but make sure you finish them all. When you've finished write down the time you took in the box above. Remember to get an adult to mark your answers, then write down your score in the box at the top of this page as well.

You have six minutes to complete this task, so work quickly. Move on if you find any of them tricky. You can always come back to those at the end.

1 spent → pen grand → ran chasm → ?

2 boot → book tall → talk mile → ?

3 fend → gene bale → calf reel → ?

4 snore → nose spoke → pose crate → ?

5 lean → mean sear → tear gear → ?

6 great → get bland → bad spoon → ?

7 flake → lane slope → lose phase → ?

8 cart → tray calf → flay cats → ?

9 bread → bred steam → stem glean → ?

10 cure → core pure → pore sure → ?

LESSON 18 PART 1: ANSWER SHEET

Mark your answer by putting a horizontal line in one of the boxes, as in the example below.

Example 1:

- rack ▬
- tack ☐
- rake ☐
- take ☐
- cart ☐

Example 2:

- grab ☐
- garb ▬
- rage ☐
- bear ☐
- bare ☐

Example 3:

- pure ☐
- sure ▬
- true ☐
- tear ☐
- sear ☐

1
- ham ☐
- has ☐
- sham ☐
- his ☐
- him ☐

2
- tile ☐
- pile ☐
- silk ☐
- milk ☐
- mild ☐

3
- deem ☐
- reef ☐
- seen ☐
- seem ☐
- teem ☐

4
- rate ☐
- care ☐
- race ☐
- tear ☐
- cart ☐

5
- fear ☐
- hear ☐
- near ☐
- dear ☐
- tear ☐

6
- one ☐
- pen ☐
- son ☐
- pie ☐
- sip ☐

7
- have ☐
- gave ☐
- save ☐
- pace ☐
- hope ☐

8
- star ☐
- cats ☐
- case ☐
- race ☐
- stay ☐

9
- gain ☐
- lane ☐
- glare ☐
- glen ☐
- flee ☐

10
- pore ☐
- core ☐
- more ☐
- sore ☐
- lore ☐

How Did You Do? Let's Find Out!

Remember, there is no self-marking in this book. Please get an adult to mark your answers.

If you scored between 7 and 10

This is terrific! Now move on to the next set of questions and try to continue your good work. Remember to check over any questions you got wrong.

If you scored fewer than 7 out of 10

⇨ Make sure that you figure out the patterns carefully by checking the letters and looking closely for changes which have happened in both the first and second pairs of words.

⇨ Do you understand what you have to do? If not, ask an adult to read the instructions and go through the examples with you again.

⇨ Make sure you work out how the words in the first two pairs of words are related, and <u>then</u> work out the third pair in the same way.

LESSON 18 PART 2

My Time

My Score

Now look at the questions below. Try to do each one as quickly as you can, but make sure you finish them all. Then write down the time you took in the box above. Get an adult to mark your answers, then write down your score in the box at the top of this page.

You have six minutes to complete this task, so work quickly. Move on if you find any really tricky. You can always come back to those at the end.

1. click → clip   slick → slip   shock → ?
2. rend → rang   bend → bang   send → ?
3. store → toe   spine → pie   sheen → ?
4. spore → rose   chime → mice   grace → ?
5. frown → gown   speak → teak   crash → ?
6. child → hid   spout → pot   chart → ?
7. soon → nose   room → more   roof → ?
8. wind → winch   rid → rich   lard → ?
9. hoped → hopped   taped → tapped   robed → ?
10. take → steak   tale → steal   pare → ?

LESSON 18 PART 2: ANSWER SHEET

Mark your answer by putting a horizontal line in one of the boxes, as in the examples below.

Example 1:

```
rack ▬
tack ☐
rake ☐
take ☐
cart ☐
```

Example 2:

```
grab ☐
garb ▬
rage ☐
bear ☐
bare ☐
```

Example 3:

```
pure ☐
sure ▬
true ☐
tear ☐
sear ☐
```

1
```
shop ☐
hop  ☐
pop  ☐
mop  ☐
top  ☐
```

2
```
sent ☐
sand ☐
sane ☐
sank ☐
sang ☐
```

3
```
her ☐
hen ☐
pen ☐
red ☐
see ☐
```

4
```
care ☐
bare ☐
wage ☐
sage ☐
cage ☐
```

5
```
rash ☐
cash ☐
dash ☐
rush ☐
dish ☐
```

6
```
car ☐
cat ☐
hat ☐
rat ☐
tar ☐
```

7
```
fore ☐
free ☐
fear ☐
lore ☐
more ☐
```

8
```
march ☐
parch ☐
larch ☐
arch  ☐
lurch ☐
```

9
```
rabble ☐
rubbed ☐
ribbed ☐
rubble ☐
robbed ☐
```

10
```
spar  ☐
spare ☐
peers ☐
pears ☐
spear ☐
```

LESSON 19 Finding the Second Word Using Those Outside the Brackets

In this exercise, you're given two sets of words. You'll need to look at the two words outside the brackets in the first set and work out how the word inside the bracket is formed. Then you'll use this information to work out the word that should go inside the brackets in the second set of words. These questions can be quite tricky so take care. Usually you'll need to take two letters from the first word and two from the second to form a four letter word inside the brackets. Let's look at an example.

Example

beam (bent) want   flop (_ _ _ _) seat

⇨ In this example, you can see that the first two letters of the first word 'beam' have been used to make the first half of the word 'bent' inside the brackets.

⇨ This must be true because the other word on the outside of the brackets is 'want' and this doesn't have a 'b' or an 'e'. But it does have the letters that make up the second part of the word – 'want'.

⇨ Using this knowledge you can now make the missing word in the same way.

⇨ So you must use the first two letters from 'flop' and the last two from 'seat', to find the missing word which is flat.

⇨ Remember each missing word is usually four letters long.

HELPFUL HINT

Sometimes a question can be particularly tricky when both words outside the brackets share letters. In this case you need to work out all the possibilities then choose the correct one. Do this by numbering each letter of the words outside the brackets. Take a look at the example below:

Number the letters on the left of the brackets 1–4 and the letters on the right 5–8. Then look at the word in brackets and write the numbers that correspond to its letters above it. Now write the same number sequence above the four blanks in brackets in the second set of words.

1 2 3 4   5 2/7 6 4   5 6 7 8   1 2 3 4   5 2/7 6 4   5 6 7 8
S A N K   (D A R K)   D R A G   F E L T   (_ _ _ _)   N A I L

The second letter is tricky to pinpoint as you don't know whether to use the second letter from the word on the left (number 2) or the third letter from the word right (number 7) as both are 'A's. In this case you should complete letters that you are sure of first. You find that the missing word looks like this:

(N __ A T)

The choices you have now for the missing letter are either E (letter number 2) or I (letter number 7). E is the correct answer since this spells the word N E A T.

LESSON 19 PART 1

My Time

My Score

Now work through the questions below. When you've finished write down the time you took in the box above. Remember to get an adult to mark your answers, then write down your score in the other box at the top of this page.

You have six minutes to complete this task, so work quickly. Move on if you find any questions tricky. You can always come back to those at the end.

1 team (tell) well   rain (_ _ _) wage

2 bore (rest) stop   bath (_ _ _) isle

3 clap (late) step   drop (_ _ _) wade

4 raid (door) pool   rash (_ _ _) tear

5 gate (page) pear   dare (_ _ _) rail

6 cone (cost) last   span (_ _ _) slot

7 tank (thin) chip   reap (_ _ _) note

8 fine (neat) path   live (_ _ _) pint

9 slip (life) feed   shin (_ _ _) rent

10 skip (pile) keel   self (_ _ _) wide

LESSON 19 PART 1: ANSWER SHEET

Mark your answer by putting a horizontal line in one of the boxes, as in the example below.

Example:

flea ☐
peat ☐
flat ▬
atop ☐
feat ☐

1
gear ☐
warn ☐
rage ☐
ware ☐
gain ☐

2
this ☐
slit ☐
slot ☐
last ☐
stab ☐

3
wear ☐
ward ☐
dear ☐
draw ☐
road ☐

4
hear ☐
heat ☐
seat ☐
sear ☐
heap ☐

5
real ☐
deal ☐
rile ☐
ride ☐
raid ☐

6
slop ☐
slap ☐
post ☐
spot ☐
past ☐

7
rota ☐
part ☐
port ☐
rope ☐
rate ☐

8
vine ☐
vein ☐
pine ☐
line ☐
pile ☐

9
sent ☐
hint ☐
hire ☐
rest ☐
rent ☐

10
side ☐
file ☐
flew ☐
life ☐
fled ☐

How Did You Do? Let's Find Out!

Remember, there is no self-marking in this book. Please get an adult to mark your answers.

If you scored between 7 and 10

A good result, well done! Move on to the next set of questions to try to continue your good work. But do check over any questions you got wrong.

If you scored fewer than 7 out of 10

⇨ Make sure you work out how the first word in brackets was made before you try to work out the second.

⇨ Do you understand what you have to do? If not, ask an adult to read the instructions and go through the example with you again.

> **TIP FOR SPEEDING UP**
>
> Make sure you only use the numbering system on questions you are finding really tricky – most of the time it is quicker to work out each letter as you go in the normal way.

LESSON 19 PART 2

My Time

My Score

Now look at the questions below. Try to do each one as quickly as you can, but make sure you finish them all. When you've finished write down the time you took in the box above. Get an adult to mark your answers, then write down your score in the box at the top of this page as well.

You have six minutes to complete this task, so work quickly. Move on if you find any tricky. You can always come back to them at the end.

1. cold (pole) cape   done (_ _ _) cube

2. stun (cats) cake   need (_ _ _) beat

3. fast (rash) rich   trap (_ _ _) glib

4. wind (fund) full   glow (_ _ _) grip

5. nice (cure) rung   best (_ _ _) limp

6. grim (mint) nest   tour (_ _ _) such

7. fake (kite) with   bald (_ _ _) pane

8. tire (true) grub   pale (_ _ _) burn

9. link (pick) pace   dive (_ _ _) dank

10. ramp (came) cove   lump (_ _ _) deep

LESSON 19 PART 2: ANSWER SHEET

Mark your answer by putting a horizontal line in one of the boxes, as in the example below.

Example:

flea ☐
peat ☐
flat ▬
atop ☐
feat ☐

1
code ☐
cone ☐
bone ☐
bond ☐
bend ☐

2
beam ☐
bean ☐
been ☐
meet ☐
meat ☐

3
tail ☐
grab ☐
garb ☐
brag ☐
rail ☐

4
limp ☐
romp ☐
loop ☐
grow ☐
poor ☐

5
slip ☐
belt ☐
slit ☐
silt ☐
bets ☐

6
shut ☐
hour ☐
sour ☐
crust ☐
rush ☐

7
pale ☐
band ☐
lane ☐
land ☐
bale ☐

8
lure ☐
pear ☐
plan ☐
pure ☐
earn ☐

9
vine ☐
vein ☐
dine ☐
dean ☐
dead ☐

10
dump ☐
mule ☐
duel ☐
deem ☐
mull ☐

LESSON 20 Using the Numbers Outside the Brackets to Find the One Inside

In this exercise, you'll need to look at the numbers outside the brackets in the first two sets of numbers and work out how they are used to make the number inside the brackets. Then you'll use this information to find the number that should go inside the brackets in the third set of numbers.

Let's look at an example.

Example

3 (6) 2   4 (12) 3   5 (?) 4

Looking carefully at the first set of numbers you can see that if the numbers outside the brackets are multiplied together, the answer is 6: 3 × 2 = 6. If you try this with the second set and you can see that 4 × 3 = 12.

Great, you've solved it – you know that you must multiply the numbers on the outside to find the answer on the inside. In the last set 5 × 4 = <u>20</u>. So <u>20</u> is the answer to mark on your answer grid.

HELPFUL HINTS

- The number inside the brackets <u>must</u> be found in <u>the same way</u> for the first two sets of numbers. So work this out before trying to solve the third set of numbers.

- Each question is different – you may be required to multiply, divide, add or subtract, so check each question carefully to work out what you have to do.

LESSON 20 PART 1

My Time

My Score

Now look at the questions below. Try to do each one as quickly as you can. When you've finished write down the time you took in the box above. Get an adult to mark your answers, then write down your score in the box at the top of this page too.

You have six minutes to complete this task, so work quickly.

1. 3 (12) 4   7 (14) 2   6 (?) 9

2. 8 (11) 3   9 (15) 6   7 (?) 13

3. 28 (7) 4   45 (9) 5   81 (?) 3

4. 7 (19) 12   13 (24) 11   15 (?) 17

5. 11 (3) 8   15 (8) 7   6 (?) 1

6. 7 (12) 84   9 (14) 126   11 (?) 132

7. 30 (600) 20   40 (1200) 30   50 (?) 30

8. 32 (57) 25   36 (78) 42   29 (?) 53

9. 72 (18) 4   63 (21) 3   55 (?) 5

10. 13 (1) 13   42 (7) 6   144 (?) 36

LESSON 20 PART 1: ANSWER SHEET

Mark your answer by putting a horizontal line in one of the boxes, as in the example below.

Example:

10 ☐
15 ☐
20 ▬
25 ☐
30 ☐

1
- 15 ☐
- 45 ☐
- 54 ☐
- 3 ☐
- 56 ☐

2
- 91 ☐
- 20 ☐
- 6 ☐
- 2 ☐
- 83 ☐

3
- 78 ☐
- 84 ☐
- 243 ☐
- 9 ☐
- 27 ☐

4
- 2 ☐
- 1 ☐
- 30 ☐
- 31 ☐
- 32 ☐

5
- 6 ☐
- 5 ☐
- 1 ☐
- 7 ☐
- −5 ☐

6
- 143 ☐
- 121 ☐
- 11 ☐
- 10 ☐
- 12 ☐

7
- 15 ☐
- 150 ☐
- 1,500 ☐
- 80 ☐
- 800 ☐

8
- 24 ☐
- 34 ☐
- 82 ☐
- 83 ☐
- 84 ☐

9
- 60 ☐
- 50 ☐
- 10 ☐
- 11 ☐
- 12 ☐

10
- 180 ☐
- 114 ☐
- 108 ☐
- 6 ☐
- 4 ☐

How Did You Do? Let's Find Out!

Remember, there is no self-marking in this book. Please get an adult to mark your answers.

If you scored between 7 and 10

This is great! Now move on to the next set of questions and try to continue your good work. But do check over any questions you got wrong.

If you scored fewer than 7 out of 10

Make sure you work out how the number in brackets was made in the first set. Then check it against the second set of numbers. If it works there too then you've found the right way. If it doesn't work for the second set, you'll have to try something else before you work out the final set.

Further hint

In the next batch of questions several of them require two steps of calculation. These can be really tough so let's look at an example first.

Example

$$4 \,(12)\, 2 \qquad 5 \,(24)\, 3 \qquad 3 \,(\,?\,)\, 4$$

In this example, you first have to add the numbers on the outside and then multiply that answer by the number on the right.

For the first set $4 + 2 = 6$, then you multiply 6 by 2 to get 12.

For the second set $5 + 3 = 8$, then you multiply 8 by 3 to get 24.

So for the final set, $3 + 4 = 7$, then you multiply 7 by 4 to get 28.

Sometimes with these questions you might even have to use a number which isn't listed, such as multiplying the two numbers on the outside and then adding 10 to the answer! If you find yourself struggling, move on and come back to the ones you found difficult.

LESSON 20 PART 2

My Time

My Score

Now look at the questions below. Try to do each one as quickly as you can, but make sure you finish them all. Remember to get an adult to mark your answers, then write down your score in the box at the top of this page. Write your time in the box above too.

You have six minutes to complete this task, so work quickly. Move on if you find any of them tricky. You can always come back to those at the end.

1   6 (12) 6   7 (16) 9   3 (?) 48

2   10 (22) 2   7 (24) 3   6 (?) 4

3   5 (30) 3   2 (28) 7   6 (?) 9

4   17 (15) 2   13 (4) 9   38 (?) 9

5   3 (19) 10   4 (26) 10   7 (?) 10

6   12 (14) 3   16 (12) 8   27 (?) 9

7   7 (11) 3   8 (13) 4   9 (?) 6

8   8 (1) 4   18 (5) 3   28 (?) 7

9   88 (22) 4   78 (39) 2   69 (?) 3

10   17 (51) 3   14 (84) 6   15 (?) 9

LESSON 20 PART 2: ANSWER SHEET

Mark your answer by putting a horizontal line in one of the boxes, as in the example below.

Example:

```
10 ☐
15 ☐
20 ▬
25 ☐
30 ☐
```

1
```
15  ☐
51  ☐
16  ☐
45  ☐
78  ☐
```

2
```
10  ☐
24  ☐
2   ☐
28  ☐
40  ☐
```

3
```
15   ☐
54   ☐
45   ☐
90   ☐
108  ☐
```

4
```
29   ☐
47   ☐
4    ☐
342  ☐
20   ☐
```

5
```
70  ☐
17  ☐
59  ☐
39  ☐
49  ☐
```

6
```
3   ☐
13  ☐
36  ☐
18  ☐
81  ☐
```

7
```
16  ☐
15  ☐
17  ☐
54  ☐
45  ☐
```

8
```
4    ☐
35   ☐
21   ☐
3    ☐
196  ☐
```

9
```
72   ☐
207  ☐
66   ☐
27   ☐
23   ☐
```

10
```
24   ☐
6    ☐
135  ☐
145  ☐
125  ☐
```

SCORE SHEET

You should have kept a score for each of the lessons in the 'My Score' box at the top of each question page. Now fill your scores for all the lessons in the table below. This will help you spot which questions you're really good at and which ones you'll need to practise further.

To convert a score out of 10 into a percentage, simply multiply your score by 10.

Lesson	Part 1 score	Part 1 percent	Part 2 score	Part 2 percent
1				
2				
3				
4				
5				
6				
7				
8				
9				
10				
11				
12				
13				
14				
15				
16				
17				
18				
19				
20				
Average				

VOCABULARY BUILDER 1
NEW WORDS

Use this page to write down any new words which you have learnt while reading this book. Use a dictionary to look up the meaning of each word and learn them!

New word	Meaning

VOCABULARY BUILDER 2
PROBLEMS TO SOLVE

1 Can you solve the problems below? Try to think of as many different meanings and spellings for words as you can and use your imagination!

The following words all have the same thing missing. What is it?

When you have found the answer, write out each word again with the missing item in the right place.

a) wed _____

b) shed _____

c) Ill _____

d) well _____

e) shell _____

f) were _____

2 Can you provide the answer to this mystery? Explain in a few sentences exactly what you think has happened and why.

'A man arrives with his car outside a hotel. He immediately knows he has lost all his money – why?'

_____
_____
_____
_____
_____

See page 126 for the answers.

REMEMBER – THESE ARE JUST FOR EXTRA PRACTISE!

VOCABULARY BUILDER 3
DIMINUTIVES

Diminutives are used to describe a smaller or younger version of something. For example, the diminutive of dog would be <u>puppy</u>. Can you find the diminutive of each noun below?

1. A young duck is a _____
2. A young goose is a _____
3. A young cow is a _____
4. A young eagle is a _____
5. A very small stream is a _____
6. A young sheep is a _____
7. A young horse is a _____
8. A young hare is a _____
9. A young goat is a _____
10. A very small river is a _____
11. A young swan is a _____
12. A young deer is a _____
13. A young tree is a _____
14. A small island is a _____
15. A young lion is a _____

gosling	cub	streamlet	cygnet	fawn
sapling	duckling	calf	islet	kid
foal	lamb	leveret	eaglet	rivulet

See page 126 for the answers.

REMEMBER – THESE ARE JUST FOR EXTRA PRACTISE!

AND FINALLY...

Firstly, let me begin by saying 'well done'. You must have worked hard to complete this book, especially on top of your other homework from school!

Now that you have completed the second verbal reasoning book in the *Practise & Pass 11+* series, it's time to take stock. Have a look back at your scores and make a note of the kinds of question you found quite straightforward and scored well on, and those that you found more difficult and didn't do so well with. Taking a verbal reasoning paper is all about strategy, so if you know you can complete some questions quickly and get them right, then you know that this will give you more time for those questions you find a bit trickier.

Make sure you read back over the methods for each question – these will serve you well during your examination. Make sure you also know which questions you can answer more quickly by using the multiple choice answer sheet to help you. When you've practised all areas of your exam and you're ready to move on, take the practice test papers in this series (*Practise & Pass 11+ Level Three: Practice Tests*).

And don't forget, if you need help with non-verbal reasoning, maths or English, there are books for each of those as well to help you prepare for your exams.

⇨ *Practise & Pass 11+ Level One: Discover English*
⇨ *Practise & Pass 11+ Level One: Discover Maths*
⇨ *Practise & Pass 11+ Level One: Discover Non-verbal Reasoning*
⇨ *Practise & Pass 11+ Level Two: Develop English*
⇨ *Practise & Pass 11+ Level Two: Develop Maths*
⇨ *Practise & Pass 11+ Level Two: Develop Non-verbal Reasoning*
⇨ *Practise & Pass 11+ Level Three: Practice Test Papers*

Keep working and good luck!

Vocabulary Builder 2 Answers
PROBLEMS TO SOLVE

1 Each word is missing an apostrophe.
  a) wed = we'd
  b) shed = she'd
  c) Ill = I'll
  d) well = we'll
  e) shell = she'll
  f) were = we're

2 The man is playing the game of Monopoly. When his playing piece (the car) arrives outside a hotel, he has landed on a property with a hotel. He cannot afford to pay the rent to the other player and so knows immediately that he has lost all his money and the game!

Vocabulary Builder 3 Answers
DIMINUTIVES

1. duckling
2. gosling
3. calf
4. eaglet
5. streamlet
6. lamb
7. foal
8. leveret
9. kid
10. rivulet
11. cygnet
12. fawn
13. sapling
14. islet
15. cub

ANSWERS

LESSON 1
1. left his, <u>this</u>
2. rolled over, <u>dove</u>
3. wife arrived, <u>fear</u>
4. smiles sweetly, <u>less</u>
5. brother after, <u>raft</u>
6. games happily, <u>mesh</u>
7. new hens, <u>when</u>
8. singing early, <u>gear</u>
9. like entering, <u>keen</u>
10. skating rink, <u>grin</u>

LESSON 2
1. imp
2. pet
3. his
4. are
5. ice
6. rat
7. art
8. ape
9. win
10. put

LESSON 3
1. b
2. g
3. b
4. k
5. l
6. t
7. w
8. h
9. m
10. d

LESSON 4
1. b
2. y
3. p
4. e
5. n
6. l
7. o
8. r
9. s
10. w

LESSON 5
1. k
2. e
3. l
4. g
5. m
6. t
7. w
8. d
9. h
10. s

LESSON 6
1. cup board, <u>cupboard</u>
2. war den, <u>warden</u>
3. than king, <u>thanking</u>
4. men ace, <u>menace</u>
5. bar rage, <u>barrage</u>
6. thank less, <u>thankless</u>
7. draw bridge, <u>drawbridge</u>
8. tree house, <u>treehouse</u>
9. ramp age, <u>rampage</u>
10. nest led, <u>nestled</u>

LESSON 7: part 1
1. bitter — sweet
2. depart — arrive
3. testing — easy
4. truth — fiction
5. glossy — dull
6. identical — different
7. delayed — punctual
8. giggle — sob
9. harsh — tender
10. muffled — clear

LESSON 7: part 2
1. nibble — gobble
2. success — failure
3. supply — withold
4. craggy — smooth
5. cheerful — miserable
6. squat — tall
7. sloppy — solid
8. commence — complete
9. permitted — forbidden
10. stain — clean

LESSON 8: part 1
1. trail
2. book
3. digit
4. case
5. catch
6. gift
7. even
8. ferry
9. jot
10. keep

LESSON 8: part 2
1. mail
2. pack
3. picture
4. raise
5. range
6. sack
7. secure
8. show
9. spare
10. tablet

LESSON 9
1. Q
2. F
3. P
4. F
5. U
6. E
7. L
8. N
9. RQ
10. WXY

LESSON 10: part 1
1. 21
2. 26
3. 47
4. 18
5. 47
6. 30
7. 3
8. 2
9. Carlton
10. Hamish

LESSON 10: part 2
1. 17
2. 20
3. 14
4. 3
5. Cecil
6. 3
7. Cecil
8. Fred/Cecil
9. Barnaby
10. 11.25

LESSON 11
1. GZMC
2. SAND
3. EKUX
4. POINT
5. WALL
6. NUTS
7. NIP
8. WRAP
9. GIVE
10. 3 W 18 N

LESSON 12
1. 21
2. 54
3. 29
4. 16
5. 486
6. 9
7. 46
8. 882
9. 2.94
10. 18

LESSON 13: part 1
1. 2
2. 11
3. 5
4. 9
5. 7
6. 12
7. 4
8. 52
9. 3
10. 25

LESSON 13: part 2
1. 3
2. 11
3. 2
4. 12
5. 6
6. 13
7. 2
8. 18
9. 4
10. 6

LESSON 14
1. U
2. P
3. W
4. X
5. O
6. KJ
7. GI
8. YB
9. RP
10. MN

LESSON 15
1. liquid   book
2. photograph toast
3. bark   hiss
4. week   year
5. distance   weight
6. books   meat
7. ship   train
8. stop   pets
9. fox   ox
10. low   broad

LESSON 16: part 1
1. minute   far
2. tiny   beautiful
3. retreat   negotiate
4. hurried   sweaty
5. servant   humble
6. wall   field
7. stroke   listen
8. whisper   fly
9. cliff   beach
10. tile   road

LESSON 16: part 2
1. fox   bear
2. rectangle triangle
3. pineapple chicken
4. house   key
5. clothes   wool
6. open   loose
7. angle   degrees
8. humid   windy
9. 80   20
10. plain   spotless

LESSON 17: part 1
1. 71529
2. 52192
3. 951729
4. EAST
5. TREES
6. TEST
7. 168114
8. 41186
9. 64381
10. 83416

LESSON 17: part 2
1. STIFLE
2. FEATS
3. LIFTS
4. STEAL
5. 1254151
6. 1423
7. 24351
8. TRADE
9. TAR
10. DEAD

LESSON 18: part 1
1. has
2. milk
3. seem
4. race
5. hear
6. son
7. have
8. stay
9. glen
10. sore

LESSON 18: part 2
1. shop
2. sang
3. hen
4. cage
5. dash
6. hat
7. fore
8. larch
9. robbed
10. spear

LESSON 19: part 1
1. rage
2. this
3. road
4. hear
5. ride
6. spot
7. rota
8. vein
9. hire
10. fled

LESSON 19: part 2
1. bone
2. been
3. grab
4. grow
5. silt
6. rush
7. land
8. pure
9. dine
10. dump

LESSON 20: part 1
1. 54
2. 20
3. 27
4. 32
5. 5
6. 12
7. 1,500
8. 82
9. 11
10. 4

LESSON 20: part 2
1. 51
2. 28
3. 108
4. 29
5. 59
6. 13
7. 16
8. 3
9. 23
10. 135